Pianta Su
Ski like the Best

Pianta Su
Ski like the Best

BY Ruedi Bear

A Sports Illustrated Book
Little, Brown and Company
Boston | Toronto

First Edition

T11/76

Photography credits will be found on page 160.

Library of Congress Cataloging in Publication Data

Bear, Ruedi.
   Pianta su : ski like the best.

   "A Sports illustrated book."
   Bibliography: p.
   1. Skis and skiing. 2. Ski racing. I. Title.
GV854.B353   796.9'3   76-22660
ISBN 0-316-08550-2

SPORTS ILLUSTRATED BOOKS
ARE PUBLISHED BY
LITTLE, BROWN AND COMPANY
IN ASSOCIATION WITH
SPORTS ILLUSTRATED MAGAZINE

Published simultaneously in Canada by Little, Brown & Company (Canada) Limited

Printed in the United States of America

For Leith

"Pianta Su"

Last summer my wife Leith and I trained a bunch of top American and Canadian racers high up in the Italian alps in a little place called Alagna. At the same time about twenty little Italian snow devils arrived, none of them more than fourteen years old. They represented the Italian Junior National Team.

I've rarely seen youngsters as eager, spirited, and funny. Their coaches resembled them in spirit and emotional behavior. To say the least, you could hear them. For two weeks we heard them yelling and shouting, "Pianta su, Pianta su, Pianta su," at their little kids in rhythmic and sometimes even dramatic voices. "Pianta su": what the hell does that mean? we asked ourselves.

The kids made astonishing progress, and we took a look in the dictionary: *Pianta* — plant, and *Su* — up. That means they were yelling at the kids, "Plant up." "Pianta" was the signal to plant the pole at the end of the curve, and "su" for up-unweighting to get off the edges and then either to step, or to set a lightly weighted edge, for the next curve. It was one of the most impressive lessons I ever had as a coach.

Author's Note

At the beginning of January 1975 I arrived in Zurich, Switzerland. I bought Europe's smallest car, a Citroën with a two-horsepower engine, and off I went along the World Cup circuit with my new vehicle. I figured it was the cheapest way to accomplish what I had in mind. When I returned to the U.S.A. in March, I had put about 10,000 kilometers on those wheels. In the meantime, I visited all the major international races and worked with the best photographers who followed the World Cup. A warm sleeping bag proved to be a great investment. At this point I would like to thank all the nice people who put me up for a day or two.

Before I decided to write this book, I had a meeting with Little, Brown and Company in Boston and met their editor, Mr. Charles Everitt. He gave me encouragement for my undertaking and said that he was seriously interested in publishing a book to grow out of a small booklet I had written, called "Technical Outlines for Ski Racing," for my Italian racing camp. My wife, the former Leith Lende, also a member of the U.S. ski team, was my greatest inspiration and help when I finally took on the challenge of putting this book together. Thank you, Leith!

While I traveled along the World Cup route, I was amazed at how many new impressions I had. I realized that when I was actively coaching I just never found the time to watch the racers as carefully as I could now. Working as a coach, I just had too many things to worry about, but now I could completely concentrate on the racers' performances. Fortunately I found most of my views confirmed, and my main goal became shooting the photographs to illustrate the technical text.

At this point I would like to mention that my thoughts and ideas are certainly influenced by many other works of current ski literature. Over the years I have studied many books on skiing, sports psychology, and physical fitness, and read hundreds of articles in ski magazines. A big influence on the way I look at ski technique came from studying the books and writings of Mr. Karl Gamma, president of the International Ski Instructors Association and head of the Swiss Ski School. I would like to thank Mr. Gamma for the help he gave me when I visited him to discuss my new ideas, views, and photo material for this book.

I would also like to express my gratitude to the following three great photographers, who were willing to let me use some of their best photos and photo sequences. Their names are: Mr. Dölf Preisig, Zurich, Switzerland; Mr. Aldo Martinuzzi, Milan, Italy; and Mr. Jürgen Kemmler, Munich, Germany. Furthermore, I would like to thank Armin Scheurer and Urs Weber, teachers at the Federal Sports School of Switzerland in Magglingen, where I graduated. Of great help to me was Ernst Bolliger, with his specific technical advice when I was working with a 35 mm movie camera. Great appreciation and many thanks go to Ernst and Ursula Hiestand in Zurich and to Claudia Schneider, who spent many hours in the darkroom developing my photo material.

When I was writing the mental part, the exciting discussions with Dolph Kuss, the former Olympic Nordic coach and current Fort Lewis College ski coach, were of great help to me. The world class racer with whom I had the closest communication while writing this book was U.S. Ski Team member Greg Jones. Many thanks, Greg!

I would also like to thank all the other racers I talked with and the many unnamed coaches I have argued about ski racing and exchanged thoughts with.

Special thanks to the British women's team, whom I had the pleasure to take to the World Championships at St. Moritz in 1974 as their coach. Most of all, thanks to all the racers I ever worked with.

I feel deep gratitude toward Dr. Guido Piderman, Zurich.

Last, but not least, and for many reasons, thanks to my mother.

The list of people I could name here and thank for their help could go on for a few more pages. For those of you who belong to this group, I would like to say: "Thanks a lot; I really appreciated your help!"

Contents

Pianta Su
Ski like the Best

COPPER
MOUNTAIN

START

1976 NATIONAL ALPINE CHAMPIONSHIPS

What It's All About

In this book, *Pianta Su: Ski like the Best,* I will describe and show you with photographs how today's best skiers are skiing. At the same time, I want to help you improve your own skiing by taking advantage of the techniques used by the best racers, such as Gustavo Thoeni, Piero Gros, Bernhard Russi, Franz Klammer, Steve and Phil Mahre, Ingemar Stenmark, Rosi Mittermaier, and Cindy Nelson. It's my goal that anyone, from the advanced intermediate skier to the expert, ski instructors and coaches, from the junior racer to the veteran racer, and even top international competitors, can enjoy this book. I realize that it's a somewhat high goal. On the other hand, I am convinced that just the photos and photo sequences will inspire you and help you improve your own skiing. Indeed, it is impossible to describe only with words what's going on technically and mechanically when a good skier skis down a mountain. Therefore the photos play at least as important a role as the text. Really young racers may even look only at the pictures, and it can still help them. It would help if you have some knowledge about ski technique from other books, magazine articles, your ski instructor, or your coach. However, you certainly don't have

15

Andy Mill, Aspen, Colorado

Gustavo Thoeni

to be an expert on ski theory to understand this book. Here I will let you know what I myself feel when skiing, and what I've heard when I asked the best racers in the world, "How do you turn them?" You will get to know the feelings and thoughts that a good skier has when he skis.

In the chapter on technique I will also explain quite a few technical principles. But I'm trying to do this in a relatively simple way. In fact, I feel it is nearly impossible to relate personally to the extremely complicated findings of a purely scientific analysis.

To see Gustavo Thoeni ski through a difficult slalom is a beautiful show. The power and force and the physical and mental skill behind Gustavo's skiing are unbelievable. He is absolutely fit. If you are really interested in skiing this way or in just skiing really well, it is to a great extent a question of how fit you are. You can ski only as well as your physical condition permits. In the chapter on conditioning, I will explain how skiers and racers can get in top shape. Only with a fit body and a good technique will a competitor be able to develop a good mind for racing. In the chapter "The Racer's Mind" I describe the life of the top ski racers and the psychological problems racers of all ages and abilities must face. What is a racer's world and what are his motivations? What kind of values does ski racing teach you? How about racing and education? Feelings, the way you think about skiing in a practical sense, and your mental preparation are as important as plain technique and physical fitness. Indeed, really to ski well you have to develop all of the above-mentioned abilities with equal care and enthusiasm.

Technique

To begin with, I would like to point out a few things and tell you about some examples which seem of great importance to me. First of all, you must be very careful not to ski with a one-track mind, with only one particular image on your mind. When you ski never get locked into any kind of firm position. Ski racing is a very dynamic sport, and it would be disastrous for your skiing if you were to get into static positions only because you try to look like one of your favorite photographs. Always imagine the photographs in this book as part of an action, as a continuing motion. You may try the way a certain position feels by leaning on some furniture in your living room. However, always realize that each of these ski photos represents only how a racer looked in a particular situation for a split second. If you teach yourself to study photographs this way you can really benefit from them.

To become a great skier you must be able to turn your skis by using many different technical principles such as counterrotation, rotation, up-unweighting, down-unweighting, and so on. Constant adaptation to the immediate situation by using the right technical mechanics **19**

Four-year-old Serge Baer of Switzerland.

is the high art of skiing. Gustavo Thoeni is the absolute master of this art. As a young kid he was just another great talent. But later he worked extremely hard on fine technical details. Today he is the finest skier on the World Cup circuit and is almost always aware of what he is doing. He is extremely well coordinated in every sense of the word and is very explosive. Besides having great natural abilities he has mobilized almost his full potential by a very imaginative training program and great discipline. Gustavo and I have crossed paths many times, and year after year he has surprised me with a further development of his already great technique.

His way of skiing has a great influence on this book, and I would like to express my special thanks to him at this point. In a time of total specialization among the best racers, he is the only racer on the World Cup who skis absolutely world class in all three disciplines: downhill, giant slalom, and slalom. Nevertheless, Gustavo remains a modest young man who never took particular joy in the crowds who celebrated and admired him as a hero after he won a race. He loves skiing and takes time out for free skiing where he really "gets it on." Away from the arena, the crowds, and the gates, he goes out for a date with the mountain. That's the real Gustavo Thoeni, one of the greatest skiers ever. He believes that fast and technically good free skiing is most important for him to keep in shape during the racing season.

I really would advise you to go out and free ski whenever you find time, just like he does! Constantly work on your technique, and observe, criticize, and analyze it. A good technical base saves a lot of hassles and makes it possible for you to ski full-out, loose, and free of compulsion when racing. Only if your technique is well established can you really give everything in a course. A racer who makes bad technical mistakes is frustrated and sometimes may think about his problems even while competing. The only way to avoid belonging to this group of racers is hard and smart work while training.

Skiing is certainly not the most natural sport. Therefore you will have to learn a number of motions that will feel funny to you at the beginning. As a young racer you have to get to know the technical and mechanical basics of ski racing. Also very important at a young age is the skiing-oriented physical development of your body. It is important that you train with love, spirit, enthusiasm, and from your own desire. It takes discipline to correct mistakes and to learn to ski economically and fast. But it sure is fun. I know you can do it if you are concentrating enough and bring up the dedication for the hard work it takes to become a really excellent racer.

This chapter on ski racing technique is not an answer to all the questions about ski racing. I want to help you and inspire you with this book to keep searching on your own. Today's top racers ski supremely well, but their technique is still developing. Every year of competition brings slight changes in equipment and technique, and there is no end in sight. It was never my intention to pin down a certain way of skiing in this book and say, "This is it, and everything else is wrong!" This is only one way of looking at it. But I believe that my views are up-to-date now, and that you are on the right track if you follow these basics.

Last, but not least, remember: Technique is not here to control you; technique is your friend to make it easier for you. The better technique you use, the less work there is and the more power and force you can put into your skiing.

Basic Mechanical Principles

It is necessary to read this section carefully in order to enjoy the rest of this book. It's the minimum you must know about ski mechanics.

Inertia:

This is the force that keeps a moving object moving in the same direction unless it is acted upon by an external force. In other words it

is the force that tends to keep your skis running in the same direction in which they are already going.

Inertia is the main force you have to deal with when you turn your skis. You need several technical motions and forces to direct the inertia of your body and skis into a new direction.

Up-unweighting:

This is one way to unweight your skis so that you can turn them. Out of a low position at the end of the curve, you perform a stretching motion (upward motion) with your legs. For a moment you will feel very little weight on your skis, and you can easily initiate the new turn. Up-unweighting is often supported by a good pole plant at the end of the curve.

Down-unweighting:

This is not a very common way to unweight anymore. However, the really good skier still applies it in certain situations every so often. From a relatively high position you sink down, decreasing the weight on your skis considerably by this motion. Particularly when you turn, by using rotation, it can be sufficient to unweight your skis by down-unweighting. Down-unweighting is most commonly used when turning over a bump, or in moguls, or when moving at very high speeds.

Counterrotation:

This is the most common way to turn your skis. The word itself explains a great deal of what's going on. It simply means that your skis turn one way and your body moves the opposite way. For instance, when you leave your body completely square (facing the fall line) when turning, you are using counterrotation. Pay attention to this: Counterrotation works properly only when your skis are nearly totally unweighted. When you ski rather slowly you have to use quite an   **23**

Here you see four world class skiers who ski very different styles, although they use the same mechanics to turn their skis. They mostly use counterrotation and they all emphasize facing "square" downhill.

extreme down-up-down motion to make a counterrotation possible and natural. The racer supported by a higher speed often can achieve the necessary unweighting with a minimum of motion.

Rotation:

This is when you turn the body and the skis in the same direction. You can use this technique particularly in very fast curves. At high speeds you can control the sliding of your skis better when you don't lose touch with the snow. Rotation also works when you have quite a bit of friction left between the skis and the snow. In heavy powder and soft snow, rotation is often a better way to make a really smooth curve. Rotation also has its disadvantages. It can easily develop into a bad habit and is often the root of the mistakes of overturning and sliding with your ski tails.

Angulation:

When you turn you must angulate with your body. Good angulation is a combination of bending the hips sideways and a forward/sideways motion of the knees. If you just lean straight inside without bending

Piero Gros en route to winning the Giant Slalom at Adelboden, 1975

your hips or knees while turning, your weight would automatically be on your inside ski. The result would be a bad curve or even a fall. The best skiers in the world, however, have considerable differences in the way they angulate. Piero Gros of Italy uses more hip motion than, for instance, Ingemar Stenmark of Sweden, who is more of a knee skier and bends his hips only slightly. To an extent it is a question of each particular skier's body build and the differences in the equipment they are using. Gros uses a boot without much forward lean. Stenmark uses a boot with an extreme forward lean. Girls in general angulate more with their hips than with their knees, which again may be the result of their body build.

Anticipation:

To anticipate a turn means that you literally start the turn with your upper body before you turn your skis. Toward the end of the turn you move your upper body toward the fall line, which helps initiate the

25

Gustavo Thoeni

new turn. Immediately afterward, you set your edges and begin your turn. Anticipating your turn has the advantage that at the beginning of your turn you already have a certain amount of inside lean, which can easily become a solid early angulation and edge-set. This way your weight and gravity point directly toward the edges, and your skis hold beautifully. Anticipating your turns is very important if you really want to ski in a modern way like the best skiers in the world. But don't mix up anticipation with rotation or even with a straight forward motion. To young racers I prefer to talk about anticipation in the following way. Seek a more direct line with your upper body than with your skis!

There are certainly many other important mechanical principles that are used in today's racing technique. However, these are the most important ones. Others will be explained and discussed in the following chapters and in the photographic analyses. I'm sure that this short introduction to ski mechanics will make it a lot easier for you to understand the rest of the technical part.

The Turn and the Body

The ideal turn is a round curve like part of a circle. In between curves there is the traverse, but in slalom and modern giant slalom the turns are usually connected.

The body position from which you start all movements is a relaxed position. You must feel your skis as completely independent units. The center of gravity is in the middle of your skis above your boots. You are standing neither too high nor too low on your skis. The lines between the shoulders, hips, knees, and boots run parallel and face horizontally downhill.

As long as you are not turning more than 45° out of the fall line you should always face horizontally downhill with the above-mentioned lines. This position is called square. See the photo of Ingemar Stenmark on the facing page. If you move these lines with the turn you are

Ingemar Stenmark of Sweden

in danger of overturning or sliding with the tails of your skis. Only when you are turning more than 45° out of the fall line does it become necessary to move these lines in the same direction as the turn.

Both legs must be totally independent and your legs and your upper body must be independent of each other, and you constantly adapt these independent units during a turn. In other words, in order to perform with the above-described neutral position you will have to ski very dynamically. In fact, the neutral square body position doesn't come by accident! If you forget about your upper body, you are most likely rotating your body slightly with the turn. This is a mistake in most cases, particularly in short turns and slalom, since it can be the beginning of overturning. The torso is an object of balance and must be kept in the most neutral position, square, horizontally facing downhill. For this reason you constantly adjust the upper body and hips by using counterrotation. Only this way will you be able to remain neutral and square while making short turns.

Anticipation is a relatively new term in skiing. Often such collective expressions lead to misunderstandings. But the word *anticipation* really describes well what happens at the end of a curve. It simply means that the body mass takes a considerably shorter line than your skis and boots do when you make a turn. You move toward the fall line with your upper body at the end of the curve. Between the old turn and the new turn, the line the center of gravity takes crosses the line the skis and boots are taking. (See the photo sequences of Cary Adgate and Ingemar Stenmark at page 52 and page 45: "The Connection.")

Before you can turn your skis you have to unweight them somehow for a split second in order to start your turn. Most of the time you up-unweight. You anticipate the turn with your upper body, up-unweight, and begin your turn, using a counterrotating motion. (See

Ingemar Stenmark

the photo of Gustavo Thoeni at page 25.) A solid pole plant supports the unweighting, unless you are skiing high speed GS or DH curves. In extremely fast curves you usually don't unweight your skis very much and are using a carefully applied rotating motion to turn your skis.

When you anticipate your turns it becomes extremely easy to angulate and set an early edge immediately after you have started the turn with your skis. Now you only have to find the right amount of angulation by bending your hips sideways and moving your knees forward and sideways. (See the photo of David Zwilling opposite.) In short turns you use less hip motion than in giant slalom-type curves. The upper body must find its perfect balancing point to compensate for the centrifugal force and inertia that are involved in a turn.

The faster a turn is, the more centrifugal force and inertia you have to compensate for. Every turn has its perfect inside lean, through angulation, which depends on the speed and radius of the turn. The faster a turn and the smaller the radius of the turn, the more extreme the angulation required. (See the photo of Piero Gros at page 9.) Never drop your head or shoulders to seek the balancing point. That's really a bad habit, since you lose the good hold of your outside ski. But many skiers have it. Despite extreme angulation you should be determined to remain as neutral and square as possible with your torso. Only in downhill may you lean a little bit with your upper body, but you still have a slight hip bend. (See the photo of Franz Klammer at page 68.)

Have your feet slightly apart in your ground position. Never lock them together! The best racers ski with their legs extremely independent and often quite wide apart, particularly when stepping in between the turns. However, being able to ski certain parts of a course, such as flushes and tight combinations, with a narrow yet still independent stance also belongs definitely to the repertory of every racer. When the best skiers in the world are free skiing they usually prefer to ski with a rather narrow stance. In fact, it's not so much the width of your stance

30

ABOVE: This is a beautiful example of an early preparation for an edge set. David Zwilling has just finished the old turn. In the air he has set both edges for the new curve before he crosses the fall line with his skis.

BELOW: Italian racer Helmut Schmalzl is shown in a sequence that documents very nicely the dynamics of an angulated pole plant, anticipation, and early edge-set.

that counts as the total independence of your legs and upper body which is important.

The absolutely ideal way to ski would be with your center of gravity always exactly centered over your skis. Your skis run the fastest this way, and you can also turn with the least effort. This is easily said, but almost impossible to perform to perfection because the angles between your skis and the slope are always changing. At this point it must be logical to everyone that when either end, the tips or the tails, is weighted with considerably more pressure, the lightly weighted area will slide. How to keep your weight centered despite terrain changes will be discussed in the section on terrain changes, snow conditions, and lines.

The Pole Plant

The *pole plant* is the trouble spot of many skiers, even relatively good ones. Many racers are not using their poles as the helpful tools they are designed to be. When you have a good pole plant you have already made a great step toward becoming a fine skier.

Theoretically most ski experts recommend planting your pole shortly before you start your turn. This is correct. However, when connecting turn after turn I believe that it is much better to think of it the following way. Plant your pole toward the end of a turn for the new curve. If you concentrate on planting your pole during the last part of a curve, when you are naturally in the lowest body position, you will pick up good timing, and you will not be too late starting the new turn. All the photo sequences illustrate this point. Never plant your pole after you start the

32

These photos were taken at the World Cup Final, 1975, at Val Gardena, Italy. Thoeni and Stenmark had exactly the same number of World Cup points going into the race. Thoeni won. Opposite, Stenmark in that race.

    The slope was extremely steep. Only racers whose legs were totally independent could handle such a steep icy slope. Below, Ingemar Stenmark demonstrates what independence between legs can really look like.

curve. Planting your pole too late is probably the most common mistake regarding the pole plant.

Plant your pole slightly angulated (at a slight angle to the snow), and with your elbow a little bit forward and inside. This way you can apply a lot of power onto your pole plant if you need it. All great racers perform their pole plants this way. Be sure not to plant your pole too close to your skis; have some space between your skis and your pole plant! In general, a good place to plant your pole is about halfway between the boots and ski tips. Carefully study the many photos, which illustrate this point clearly.

If you plant your pole in the way described above it will help you pick up good timing. Another important fact is that the pole plant serves as a "rotation axis." Furthermore, it is a great help in supporting the unweighting of your skis in many turns, particularly in slalom, in giant slalom, on the steep as well as in free skiing. See below and the photo of Gustavo Thoeni at page 36. A solid well-performed pole plant also

*Gustavo Thoeni
on his way to a Gold Medal
at St. Moritz, 1974*

supports the lateral motion when making a "lateral step" by helping with the unweighting.

Nicely timed and coordinated arm work is the key to a good pole plant. Only if you consciously prepare your pole plant during the turn will you be ready to plant it properly toward the end of the curve. Once you find the right timing for your pole plant you only have to concentrate on getting your inside arm ahead of you, particularly in courses. The inside arm should always be the first part of the body to pass a gate. This really helps you stay square to the fall line and avoid overturning.

Naturally there are situations and turns where you don't plant your pole at all. For instance, in downhill curves or in fast giant slalom turns it would not be good to plant your pole, and furthermore, you simply don't have time. You can also ski easy vertical sections in flat slaloms without planting your poles. It's a matter of feeling and sometimes tactics to recognize such parts and situations.

Leith Lende

Piero Gros, 1976 Olympic Gold Medalist, in the slalom

Pianta Su: Ski like the Best

This is Gustavo Thoeni at his best. It's the kind of skiing that brought him three world cup titles. Let's look at this sequence a little closer.

1. Gustavo is absolutely square. His inside arm is the first part of his body to pass the gate. He is well prepared for the upcoming pole plant.

2. He is planting his pole toward the end of the curve when his seat is at its naturally lowest position.

3. As you see, he uses an angulated pole plant pointed sideways/forward.

4. When you plant your pole in a slightly angulated form, like Gustavo in this sequence, you will get an automatic uplift or, in other words, an up-unweighting. Notice his great anticipation, which means he is taking a more direct line with his upper body than with his skis.

5. Look carefully and you will notice the simple down-up-down that characterizes this sequence. Here he is on his way up and simultaneously starting a counter-rotation, which only works when you have your skis completely unweighted.

6. He has set his edges lightly and as early as he could before reaching the fall line. It was very steep and icy here.

7. He leaves enough space between his ski tips and the pole not to catch his tip and enough room for the inside lean (angulation) of his body (required by the mechanical forces and inertia of the body when turning) to pass the pole. His body, however, is very aggressive.

8. He again comes down and has all his weight on his outside ski when he passes the pole. His counterrotation is just about completed and he looks way ahead. His inside arm is again the first part of his body passing the gate, and with his other arm he is well-prepared for the up-coming pole plant.

9. Reaching the end of the turn, he plants his pole again. He is anticipated and in the process of stepping and changing his weight onto the new outside ski for the next turn.

. . . and all of this in 7/10 of a second. Of course there are many other important technical characteristics which one could see in this sequence: for instance, the beautiful game of balance between center-weight and being slightly backward between gates, or the obvious assistance Gustavo gets from his pole plant as a rotation axis.

Gustavo Thoeni's second slalom run at the World Championships in St. Moritz, 1974, was one of the best performances in the history of alpine ski racing. He skied beautifully and smoothly yet risked everything . . . and made up the two seconds necessary to win the title.

The Edge-Set

Now we come to the most important and complex aspect of the turn, the edge-set. An edge-set is putting a flat ski onto an edge. Whenever you start a turn you must immediately set your edges simply by using a forward/sideways motion of your knees and ankles. Having an early edge-set makes it possible to ski a considerably flatter ski over the whole curve, smoothly and precisely. See the photo sequence of Piero Gros opposite.

In order to be able to begin a turn with an early edge-set, it is of primary importance that you anticipate the turn with your upper body first. This means that toward the end of the curve, along with a good pole plant, you seek a more direct, vertical line with your upper body than with your skis. This enables you to keep your momentum going in a straighter line than your skis. This relatively aggressive motion is essential in order to perform an early edge-set at the beginning of a turn and to step well. When you are unweighted, a split second after your pole plant, the edge-set must take place. After you anticipate a turn with your upper body in the described way, it is extremely easy to move forward/sideways with your knees onto an early edge-set. Try to keep the whole ski in touch with the snow, although sometimes it's just not possible.

How you set your edges depends a great deal on the terrain and snow conditions. Sometimes you really try to ski from the inside edge of your outside ski onto the inside edge of the new outside ski, particularly in icy medium-steep slaloms. But be careful, for this is not always fast and should not become a habit for all turns. Indeed, it's too simple to say that you always ski from one outside ski and inside edge onto the other outside ski and inside edge when turning. In flat terrain and in soft snow, it becomes necessary to apply some pressure onto your inside ski and outside edge toward the end of the turn. While I watched the best racers on the World Cup, I observed over and over again how they skied for a short moment on their inside ski and outside edge shortly after the middle of the curve. See the photo

This sequence of Piero Gros shows the edge-set in soft snow conditions. He is known to look very aggressive when competing, but when you analyze him you rarely find a racer with such a delicate touch, and feeling for snow. His balance is always superb, and look at his knees.

sequence of Ingemar Stenmark on page 44. Then they smoothly rolled their inside ski onto an early edge-set and put their weight solidly onto their outside ski again. This way, the best racers are often smoothly skiing into their step or lateral connection. In between turns, however, they often ski on totally flat skis for a short distance.

Let's go quickly back to the role of the inside ski. Never apply any weight onto the inside ski at the beginning of the curve. At this point the weight and gravity of your body must be solidly applied onto your outside ski by using the right amount of angulation. Always keep your weight fully on your outside ski until you pass the middle of the turn.

To start a curve on an entirely flat ski or without anticipation is a very bad habit. However, when you begin the curve this way you won't have any immediate problems. It is tempting to start your turn on a flat ski, because you don't realize your mistake until it's too late. Toward the middle of your turn you will get into trouble and start sliding badly, and at the end of the turn your skis will undoubtedly start chattering. There is nothing you can do about it anymore. Never take the "easy way in" by starting your curve on flat skis without anticipation. You're much better off to keep away from this bad habit and concentrate on a smooth and early edge-set.

Sometimes you may have been told by your instructor or coach, "You are on your edges too much!" However, this is a dangerous observation unless he also gives you the proper correction. Most likely you were just late with your edge-set or simply forgot to anticipate the turn with your upper body. Therefore you started sliding and compensated by overedging. By now I hope you see the logic behind an early edge-set when starting your turns. Not only will you ski better and faster this way; you can also ski with more precision and consistency.

The Lateral Connection

If he had to decide on the most significant change in alpine racing technique over the last ten years, almost every ski expert would

Rosi Mittermaier, West Germany. This sequence is excellent proof that girls are capable of skiing mechanically like the best men. Rosi prepared her pole plant well and early. She is square throughout the entire turn. She planted her pole at a slight angle just like Gustavo Thoeni and got that automatic lift. Her upper body is seeking a shorter line (anticipation) than her skis. She stepped over and beyond the imaginary vertical lines of her point of gravity. She sets her edges extremely early, a good distance before the fall line. Good turn, Rosi!

spontaneously mention the amazing and almost total use of the lateral connection, or the lateral step. All the great racers use lateral steps in most turns, particularly in slalom and giant slalom. Even the downhill racers use lateral steps in certain curves today. Are there any turns left where you don't use a lateral connection? Yes, there still are and always will be such turns. In most flushes and other vertical gate combinations, today's top racers still ski with a relatively narrow stance without using a lateral step. Usually in such situations there is simply not enough time for a step and, more important, a step just wouldn't help you pick up speed. You can lose time when you step in such gates. Never forget that the most direct line is usually the fastest, particularly in slalom, and indeed there are situations where you can overstep. However, in one important regard you still ski mechanically in the same way as when you step. Even in flushes and in vertical gates, all the best racers remain extremely independent with their legs and skis, always ready to react to either side, always ready to step when necessary.

On the whole, there is no doubt that the lateral connection is one of the most important technical skills a racer has to perfect if he wants to ski like the best racers in the world. Lateral steps come in all sizes and forms, and are used in steep, medium, and flat terrain. Therefore, it is very hard to describe the average lateral connection. Below I will go into some of the details you must know when you want to perform a good lateral step. However, there is no general guideline you can follow, since each lateral step is different according to the situation. I'm sure the following pointers will help you find the right approach for your own steps.

When you use a lateral step you make the radius of your turn considerably bigger. This enables you to ski a more vertical line, particularly when skiing through a course. This means that you create less friction by less turning and will therefore be faster than you would be without a lateral step. However, to take advantage of this principle you can and must ski a lower line than you normally would without lateral steps.

In order to perform a good step, you must set your edges very early at the beginning of the curve. This way, you will be able to build up the

Gustavo Thoeni

necessary pressure gradually throughout the whole turn. Toward the end of your turn you will feel a good hold with your outside ski and will be ready to step. If you neglect this point and start your edge-set too late, there will be too much pressure all at once at the end of your turn. This will make an efficient step impossible.

Shortly after the middle of the turn you feel the most pressure on your outside ski and your edge is holding firmly. Now it happens! As you plant your pole you release your edge by up-unweighting and simultaneously seek a more direct and vertical line with your upper body. The pole plant and anticipation are helping your step. In this split second, it is suddenly quite easy to move your upper ski uphill beyond the vertical line of your center of gravity. You then step onto the outside edge, a flat ski, or slightly onto the inside edge, depending on the situation. Your weight is centered between your left and right ski for a short moment.

To point out the most important factor again: The "key" to a good connection is the uphill lateral step of your upper ski beyond the imaginary vertical line of your center of gravity. Here it is important to mention the fact that the big mass of your body — the hips and torso — is always taking a shorter line between turns than your skis and boots do. Pay your greatest attention to this point! See "The Connection" photos opposite.

In many turns the lateral connections are almost invisible to the eye, since the best racers barely lift their skis off the ground when stepping.

Ingemar Stenmark

In fact they often literally ski into their steps by having their weight on the outside edge of their inside ski for a split second toward the end of the curve. Immediately afterward they roll their inside ski onto an early edge-set. This way, their inside ski once again becomes their outside ski and the connection is completed. This technique is used particularly in soft or grippy snow and in flat or medium terrain. See also the photo sequence of Piero Gros at page 39.

In flats and soft snow you can sometimes still use a skating motion, where you set your upper ski at an angle onto the outside edge of your inside ski. This type of skating step has been used in giant slalom for many years, and there are still situations where the best racers are using skating steps, particularly when it's flat and wide open, and also in the first gates after the start.

Today's world class racer often steps with his upper ski into a slight stem position. However, this stem position has no stem effect at all, because the momentum of your body has already taken a more direct line by anticipating the turn. In other words, your momentum is going in just about the same direction as your upper angulated ski. Particularly in medium-steep and steeper sections, racers perform their steps in the above-described way. Indeed, when you step onto a slightly stemmed ski you turn a few degrees less than if you should place your upper ski parallel to your outside ski. Obviously you are keeping your skis slightly more in the fall line, which decreases the friction encountered during the turn. Here again, it is extremely important to mention that you must anticipate your turns when doing this. Otherwise such a step would really end up as a stem christiania. See the photo sequences of Cary Adgate at page 52 and Gustavo Thoeni opposite.

After these observations, it becomes obvious how difficult it is to pin down a valid rule for the average lateral connection. In fact it is impossible, because they are performed in so many different variations. There are often situations where you can step directly onto a

Every so often you catch a racer in this position:

pointing the uphill ski immediately into the fall line after unweighting is especially effective when turning over a drop-off or a mogul, and sometimes in ruts. (See Cary Adgate, at page 52.) But don't mistake it as a special technique. It's only a way to handle a specific situation. There is no stem effect involved, since the mass of your body has already anticipated and is going in the same direction as your vertically pointed outside ski. Gustavo Thoeni is especially good at using this particular technical skill to its best advantage.

new edge-set. On the other hand, there are many other situations where it is faster and more natural to step first onto the outside edge of your upper ski or onto a flat upper ski before you roll your ski onto an early edge-set. The constantly changing terrain, the size of your turns, the different snow conditions, and the speed with which you approach a curve are all important factors which influence each lateral connection. Therefore it's to a great extent your feeling, many hours of practice, and lots of experience that will finally teach you to step efficiently in all sorts of conditions.

Terrain Changes, Snow Conditions, Different Lines

How do terrain changes and snow conditions influence your technique and your line? If you are a really good skier you must pay a great deal of attention to this question. Choosing a good line and applying the right technique is not just a matter of plain technical skill, particularly in unusual snow conditions. It certainly takes a good head too. If you really want to win races you have to be creative and have a good imagination when choosing your line and technique for the race. When you become aware of the fact that it is important to use these mental qualities, you will be able to develop them and will find the right approach more easily. In the chapter "The Racer's Mind" I will come back to this problem when I talk about tactics. But now let's look at the technical side of adaptation to the terrain and snow conditions.

In the Lauberhorn slalom at Wengen, Switzerland, I chose the upper, extremely difficult, steep, and icy wall to make my observations. It was simply incredible to see how the best world class racers turned their skis in this section. Later, I will describe the most obvious technical tendencies I observed while concentrating on "How do the best racers ski steep terrain?" The main thing is the balance factor. Your center of gravity has to be in the middle of your skis pointing in an imaginary

Ingemar Stenmark at Wengen's Lauberhorn Slalom, 1975

vertical line down toward your boots. This way the pressure is distributed over the entire ski. But that's more easily said than done! On the steep this means that you must lower your seat considerably and therefore in a way move slightly backward. Your thighs should be just about parallel to your skis. This will automatically bring your point of gravity back to the center of your skis. If you neglect this point and remain in a neutral ground position, your weight will be on your tips, and you will have no chance to hold well in the steep. Your tails would start sliding badly after the middle of your turn. At the same time, watch that you don't lose the forward angle between your knees and boots, and never hang backward onto your spoilers. See the photo sequence of Gustavo Thoeni at page 37 winning the slalom Gold Medal in the World Championship at St. Moritz on a very steep and icy hill.

Another important point on the steep is that you should use both legs completely independently. In no other situation than on the steep do you bend your knees at such completely different angles. Your inside knee is often almost entirely bent, while at the same time your outside leg is almost totally stretched out. Try this: Approach an icy steep slope in a low seat but with a solid forward angle between your boots and knees. Shortly after your pole plant you set your edges. Then as soon as you can, extend your outside leg with great power. Try to get a lot of friction immediately onto that outside ski. Simultaneously bend your inside knee a lot. I'm sure you will experience an almost sensational feeling of tremendous hold with your edges when you do this correctly for the first time. Suddenly you will be able to carve round turns even on steep icy pitches. I observed Ingemar Stenmark skiing **50** this way over and over again, and he is surely the best world class

Gustavo Thoeni, World Cup winner 1972, 1973, and 1975, Giant Slalom Olympic Gold Medal 1972, World Champion 1974 in Slalom, and Giant Slalom, combined World Champion 1976. He applies a good solid pole plant although the hill is relatively flat. He doesn't use as much up-unweighting as he does in steeper terrain. He is unweighted in the second picture and uses a counterrotation that is visible in the third picture. In the last picture of this sequence you can see his superb arm control. He has his inside arm ahead and the outside arm ready to plant toward the end of the curve.

racer on the steep. The mechanical explanation for turning with this technique on the steep is simple and logical. If you turn without applying a lot of force on a solid edge set at the beginning of the curve, your entire weight and momentum would abruptly be forced on your skis toward the end of the curve. As a result, your skis would chatter and you would lose a lot of time. See the photo sequences of Ingemar Stenmark at page 49 and Fausto Radici at page 98.

On medium steep terrain you should ski as well balanced as possible. To ski with your weight centered is not only fastest; your skis also hold the best. Only in the flat and in fast parts is it sometimes advantageous to ski slightly back of your center of gravity. However, don't overdo it! This only works in straight flat parts, a few sneak gates, and open hairpins. When you ski on the flat you must set your edges with a delicate and gentle touch. It's very important that you don't overedge on the flats. Although even here you should start your turn with an early edge-set. The main difference between skiing on flat terrain and on steep is simply in the amount of edge you use and in the power you

apply when edging. On the flats you must try to avoid as much friction as possible, and ski lightly. See the gentle edge set of six-foot-tall Piero Gros in the flat at page 39.

Whenever there are moguls and bumps, you have to stand extremely loose and centered on your skis. You have to extend and sink constantly in order to adapt to the terrain and to stay on the snow. As the friction increases skiing into a mogul, you sink gradually. Right after the top of the mogul you try to keep in touch with the snow by literally stretching out your legs. To a great extent it's a natural feeling, which you have to develop by free skiing. It is also a matter of timing and coordination. Indeed, theory doesn't help you much here. Just go out and fill in the valleys between those moguls and bumps by using a lot of up-and-down motion just like a spring.

Learn how to recognize favorable terrain for your skiing. A little unevenness can help you initiate your turn or, on the other hand, make it harder for you when you use it incorrectly. Every top racer has a fine memory and feeling for favorable and unfavorable terrain for his skiing and always adapts his lines naturally. In almost every course there are places where you should not take the most direct line and instead should take advantage of obviously favorable terrain. You may ski a little longer line but pick up some speed, making up the time in the subsequent gates. This is particularly important in downhill and giant slalom. In slalom the best racers ski more and more direct lines regardless of terrain changes. Apparently there is too little time between gates to go much out of the direct line.

On very hard snow and on ice: Here it is important that you make extremely round turns. You must set your edges very early and increase the pressure on your outside edge with feeling. This way, you will hold well and be able to use good steps of medium size.

On grippy hard snow and on hard-packed powder: You no longer need to make your turns with the biggest possible radius. Here you have to take the most direct line, and make your turns with a smaller radius. In between turns, you straighten your traverses out, and use relatively powerful and big steps. You must be determined to leave your skis as much in the fall line as possible. The good grip of your edges in these snow conditions allows a very aggressive style of skiing.

On really soft snow: Here again, you have to ski with big round curves like the ones you use on ice. It is most important that you avoid any extreme or hard edging. It's a bad mistake to ski too direct a line in soft snow. You would cause far too much friction and simply be slow. This is the reason why you must use big radius turns when it's really soft. You can also rotate slightly and use up-unweighting. Sometimes you   **53**

This is Cary Adgate of the U.S. Ski Team scoring his first World Cup Slalom points at Megève, France, 1975. He had huge ruts to deal with and overcame this handicap by using extreme up-and-down motion. In this particular gate the rut was so deep that he had to absorb a big following mogul between turns.

may even use both arms in a swinging up-motion to support the up-unweighting and stepping, but then the snow has to be almost sticky and wet. In such conditions you must use different-size steps, and always try to avoid any unnecessary friction. You should also ski with your weight on both skis when it is really soft.

Slalom

Since we have already studied the technical sides of slalom skiing in the earlier sections, I will not talk particularly about technique here. Indeed, there are many general rules every slalom racer has to know before he will become successful in this discipline.

Slalom is the event of quickness, aggression, and complete attack. Despite an aggressive attack you must ski in a soft, smooth, and supple way, always connecting your turns. No one can ski under total tension for more than twenty gates and still be fast without falling or missing a gate! Pay deliberate attention to the principle "Tension needs relaxation." Muscles that are not involved in turning should also be relaxed. The phase of relaxation is only a split second per turn, but make sure that you don't forget it. A good place to relax for a short instant is between turns when your skis are unweighted; that means in the "connection." See "The Connection" photos at page 45.

You must adapt to any rhythm changes in the course. No slalom has a regular rhythm, even when a course has a so-called "nice rhythm." You will win a lot of time if you ski a slalom exactly in its irregular rhythm. On the other hand, if you get hooked on a beat (regular rhythm), you will lose a split second in every gate, ranging from a few hundredths to as much as one to two tenths. It's easy to figure out what this means in a sixty-gate course.

You must take chances while training slalom, or your technique will soon become stale. To make five out of six runs is by far enough; even to make four out of six runs is all right during an early, intensive training period. Running thousands of gates is absolutely necessary in order to experience as many different combinations and situations as possible. You have to learn how to ski near your limits. Only this way will you develop good judgment and learn how to be consistent and fast. Never ski out of a course in training easily. Perform miracles! You will be surprised how often you are able to make an acrobatic recovery out of an almost hopeless situation. Of course you always have to be prepared for these recoveries in the back of your mind. It also takes confidence, mental strength, and a lot of practice.

Always keep your ski tips at least a foot away from a normal offset slalom gate. Many gates require leaving even more distance between the tips of your skis and the slalom pole. Only in extremely vertical gates, easy flat parts, and grippy snow conditions may you cut in slightly closer.

Let me tell you why this is so! If you ski technically well, you will slide very little when you turn. For every turn you also use a certain amount of angulation, which is usually the most extreme exactly when you pass the gate. Therefore, you must naturally leave the right amount of space for your angulated body to pass the gate. Only in this way will you be able to curve efficiently and without sliding in a course. As you already know, your heaviest part, the upper body and hips, always takes a considerably shorter line in slalom and giant slalom than your skis and boots do. A racer who does not know this basic mechanical fact and approaches all the gates within inches of his ski tips will never achieve good consistent results and will always remain a poor technician.

One more time and in one sentence: With your body you can be very aggressive in slalom and giant slalom by attacking the gates directly, yet at the same time you have to develop a fine feeling to

55

keep exactly the right distance away from the gate with your tips. Gustavo Thoeni and Piero Gros are the absolute masters of this particular point. See their photos opposite. When you see them attack a slalom they often look unbelievably aggressive, as though they wanted to demolish the entire course. But, if you watch just their skis you will be surprised how smoothly they set their edges, and how much they keep away from the gates with their ski tips, never in danger of catching a tip.

To win slaloms regularly you must be good at tactics and at studying a course! To an extent this is a psychological problem. Use your creative imagination! No one has the right to interrupt your concentration while you study a course. You must get totally into it when you climb up a course, calmly memorizing and recognizing important terrain changes, time-gaining bumps, and eventual alternatives. Only if you are able to concentrate as a young racer will you achieve some kind of a routine after a while. This routine is a great help and relief to you when you have to concentrate for the really big races.

The best slalom racers are constantly attacking full-out. Of course they don't always finish this way. But a racer simply can't hold back if he wants to place well in a top field. The best slalom racers all take great chances and risks and ski the most direct line regardless of terrain changes. A couple of spectacular recoveries are usually a part of *every* slalom victory. It takes real nerve to ski your best for two runs in an important race, particularly when you are under stress. Toni Sailer, coach of the Austrian ski team and former Olympic champion, explained the poor results of his slalom specialists in a Kitzbühel slalom like this: "To win a slalom in front of 20,000 people and TV cameras is to a great extent a psychological problem. It also takes a certain amount of 'easy-goingness' along with intense concentration if a racer really wants to ski his best in front of a critical audience. . . ." The second run of Gustavo Thoeni when he became world champion at St. Moritz in 1974 seems to confirm this theory. Gustavo commented on his victory with the following words, "After the first run I was almost

BELOW:
left, Gustavo Thoeni;
right, Piero Gros

two seconds out and in eighth place. I just didn't care anymore, and I had nothing to lose. I attacked as much as I could. I became faster and faster. It was like a dream, but somehow I made it." All the experts who saw his run agreed that they had witnessed one of the greatest slalom runs ever. His winning time was the fastest by over two seconds in this run. Indeed he risked everything and won everything.

But, talking about having nerves and keeping cool, I have to mention the great downhill run of Franz Klammer in the Olympics of 1976. Tens of thousands of Austrians had come to see "the unbeatable Franz Klammer" win. The Austrian crowd is known to be extremely tough on their athletes when they fail to win. Klammer was to run number 15, and his closest rival, Bernhard Russi of Switzerland, held a comfortable lead after an almost perfect run. The course wasn't Klammer's favorite, because he likes them less turny. The people would never forgive him for second place and he knew it. Shortly after he pulled out of the starting gate he made several mistakes and at the halfway point he was about ½ second behind Russi, a margin that few people could have made up. He skied at his outer limits and risked everything in the lower part, in one of the great downhill runs of his life. The only alternative for Franz Klammer was to win, and he did.

Giant Slalom

Giant slalom is the youngest alpine discipline. This is somewhat surprising, because it seems to many of us the most natural way of skiing. To ski down a mountain as fast as possible by using all the technical tools and imagination you have available is very similar to a giant slalom. Indeed, giant slalom is in many technical ways the most demanding and difficult event. It takes great skill and a very good feeling for adapting to the terrain and to different snow conditions. There is a little downhill and slalom in every challenging giant slalom. Elegance and smoothness paired with aggression are important ingredients of modern giant slalom racing.

58

LEFT: Phil or Steve Mahre? RIGHT: Gustavo Thoeni

Giant slalom, like slalom, has developed into an event requiring constant attack. But don't misunderstand this! Your attack must be in harmony with your conscious concentration on the terrain and on differing snow conditions. Besides being elegant and smooth, you must develop the feeling of letting the skis go out of the curve. Take advantage of favorable terrain changes to pick up speed. Don't narrow-mindedly follow the shortest line between the gates. You will soon develop a creative recognition of longer but faster lines. Giant slalom is a difficult event because you usually have to adapt several times to extreme terrain changes in a relatively short time by changing your technique in the same course. This is why you must free-ski a lot. It's the best teacher for good giant slalom skiing. Do it hard, playfully, with imagination and lots of rhythm changes. The round curve is the most significant characteristic of good giant slalom racing. In this event you must use your entire repertory of technique: rotation, counterrotation, up- and down-unweighting.

Giant slalom has more extreme rhythm changes than slalom. It is of immense importance that you memorize these changes while studying the course, and use them to your advantage. If you get hooked on a beat (regular rhythm) in giant slalom it will be even more disastrous for your time than it would be in slalom.

In high-speed parts, make sure to ski in a low position, wherever it is possible, for aerodynamic reasons. See the section "Downhill." But

Eric Haker, Norway

Steve and Phil Mahre are twins, and they are just about equally good. This sequence shows Phil Mahre on his way to fifth place in the Olympic giant slalom in 1976. Phil and Steve both ski with a very modern technique, both anticipate their turns beautifully. They also use a lot of "up and down," which they support by their arm motion.

be very careful not to overdo it. Usually there are only a few seconds in each giant slalom where you may use a downhill position, but when it's possible it always pays off. Never remain in a tuck or low downhill position when the turns require difficult technical motions.

Here, too, you must leave the right amount of space between your ski tips and the gate. In giant slalom this space can be as big as two feet in extreme situations. In the flats and in more vertical gates you may take more chances and approach the gates slightly closer. A misjudgment when choosing your line or in your approach to the whole course can easily cost you three to five seconds in a difficult giant slalom without your having made any other particular mistakes. Indeed, finding and holding the right line are two of the most important points in giant slalom. Therefore the section "Terrain Changes, Snow Conditions, Different Lines," (page 48) is of great value and should be studied carefully by the giant slalom specialists among you.

The lateral step has been used regularly in giant slalom since the 1968 Winter Olympics, when Jean-Claude Killy used more steps than there were gates during his great and overwhelming giant slalom victory. The late Roger Staub was an extreme stepper. He won the giant slalom in the 1960 Olympics at Squaw Valley. Because of the great importance of the lateral step you should read about its technical aspects in the earlier section "The Lateral Connection." All other technically important aspects of giant slalom racing have already been described in earlier sections.

Downhill

Downhill is the event which probably takes the most natural ability, although there are, and always were, a number of top down-hillers who weren't that good in the other disciplines. They usually are

62

Franz Klammer

quite big and heavy, and their size and weight may have a certain influence on their specialization, because they are often obviously handicapped in slalom and giant slalom. On the other hand, I believe strongly that it isn't necessary to be big and heavy to develop into a top downhiller. There are plenty of people who have proved the contrary. One thing however seems to be a fact: you must enjoy it. Downhillers must have an opportunity to train downhill often, which is a problem for almost all racers except those who grow up or live in a big alpine ski resort.

Now let me tell you some of the most important points you must think of when practicing or racing downhill. This section will be slightly longer, since I will go into specific technical details of downhill racing which I could not cover in the earlier sections.

First you must choose the terrain. When training for speed, use rather easy, medium, and flat terrain. Here you can practice the ideal DH position. If you are practicing turns, you may use steeper sections and ski huge giant slalom turns at the highest possible speed. Train early in the morning or late in the afternoon, when there are not many people on the slopes. A friend who signals where and when the *piste* is free can be a great help. Always study the terrain thoroughly, in order to protect yourself and others from unnecessary accidents. Notice alternative spots where you could stop or ski out in emergency situations. Make it a rule never to train downhill in unfamiliar terrain. In Switzerland, France, Italy, Austria, and in quite a few places in the U.S.A. and Canada you may train downhill alone if you stick closely to the described rules. Many of the great downhillers have done it this way!

It is neither necessary nor good to go as straight as possible everywhere you can. Instead, develop a feeling for finding smooth lines where you let your skis run as flat as possible and with great sensitivity. Train on flats often and for hours, even if it becomes boring sometimes. Develop a good feeling for having equal weight on both

Franz Klammer

The Hahnenkamm Downhill in Kitzbühel is without a doubt the most popular alpine ski race in the world. The finish is a steep schuss almost a mile long. Each year huge crowds gather along the piste carrying big posters and banners with the names of their favorites. The Swiss neighbors usually send a contingent of fans carrying cowbells and Swiss flags. The atmosphere is incredibly tense and excited by the time the race starts. It is almost a certainty that each year one or two racers in the top 30 will crash in the fastest section of the race as they come into sight. A fall of this speed is an absolutely terrifying show. (See Page 76.)

Around 25,000 people watched this scene live, and a few million were watching on TV. Rolland Collombin had the lead, and the hopes of the crowd were with Franz Klammer (above). It was the last race before the World Championships at St. Moritz. The racers came into the last schuss at 135 km/hr. There is a big bump if a racer comes too low into the last gate. Klammer barely made this gate and took an incredible flight (above right). Recovery looked absolutely impossible. The crowd was shocked. A split second later he was on his way toward the finish gate in a low tuck. He reminded me of a cat that falls from a tree and runs away. Klammer finished in second place three-tenths of a second behind Collombin, to the wild cheers of the crowd.

skis and equally distributed over the entire ski. Only in this way will you become an excellent glider.

In all DH races there are certain key points. For example: If there is a difficult steep schuss and a tricky bump before a long flat, you have to ski this section at the highest possible risk, measured by your own personal possibilities, and in the lowestposition you can. This way, you will hit the following flat with a higher speed and win seconds. If you backed out on the steep and going over the bump, even the best tuck won't help you much in the flat part. Indeed, you can lose a DH race within sixty feet!

During long difficult high-speed curves, you must concentrate on absorbing all the little uneven changes and bumps in the terrain while continuing your turn. You always feel a little shaky in every downhill; even the best skiers do sometimes. You feel like you are always in the air and get angry and afraid occasionally, but everyone faces the same problem. To be in the air often is the nature of downhill. The most courageous downhiller is not free of fear, and often it takes a lot of willpower and courage to overcome it.

The typical downhill curve also has slightly different mechanical basics from high-speed giant slalom turns. In GS your angulation is achieved by a relatively big hip bend sideways, and your shoulders and upper body are kept in a square position. This is not true in downhill curves. Although the angulation is often extreme, you must get the required inside lean with much less hip bend. The knees form a good forward/sideways angle, but the hips are only slightly bent. The rest of your angulation comes through a straight inside lean. Your upper body is no longer square and leans slightly toward the turn. However, don't drop your head inside. You must have your weight solidly on your outside ski, and you often must bend your inside knee deeply. You also usually use a slight rotation motion and keep in touch with the snow.

Cindy Nelson, Olympic Bronze Medal Winner, 1976. At Grindelwald in 1973 Cindy Nelson broke the ice by beating three-time World Cup winner Annemarie Proell. Previously Annemarie had a winning streak of 12 consecutive World Cup downhill victories. Two years before her victory over Annemarie at Grindelwald, Cindy had broken her leg on the same downhill course.

Franz Klammer
on and off the snow

Up-unweighting is seldom used in DH. When you lose contact with the snow in a downhill curve, you must pay great attention to the following point. Keep your angulation despite being in the air! Don't start to change your position, because by the time you land again you will need this angulation. Turning well in downhill is also to a great extent a matter of your psychological preparation and many years of practical exposure to fast downhills.

Which downhill position is the fastest? Let's discuss some results from the wind tunnel experiments of the Swiss Ski Team. (I was personally the test racer during the first test program in the Swiss Air Force wind tunnel.) Let's concentrate on an example that I figured out from the official results. We used a test section of 30 meters simulated in the wind tunnel at a speed of 90 km/hr. After their mathematical evaluations of the results, the scientists came to the following conclu-

Bernhard Russi experimenting with the ideal downhill position in the wind tunnel of the Swiss Army at Emmen, Switzerland. The wind tunnel is designed to test airplane aerodynamics. Instead of a moving object against air, it's the air that is blown through the tunnel at very high speeds toward a standing object. Highly sophisticated precision instruments measure the value of wind resistance caused by the object.

sion. A perfect DH position performed at 90 km/hr over the distance of 30 meters was about two tenths of a second faster than a higher but still relatively low position with the arms forward/sideways out to help with balance. In addition to the loss of two tenths of a second over such a short distance, the racer will lose an amount of momentum. If there were a long easy flat following such a test section, you would undoubtedly lose several seconds because of backing out during the "hairy" section of 30 meters, approximately 100 feet.

If you had concentrated fully for those 100 feet and approached them well balanced and with the necessary courage, you most probably could have overcome your fear of skiing such a key point in a relatively low downhill position. See the photomontage at page 73, top. This example, however, should not encourage you to try the "impossible." Too many young racers have ended their careers by foolish misjudgments of their own limits. On the other hand, if you really want to become a top downhiller, you have to explore intelligently the outer regions of your possibilities. Only through experience and many fast DH miles will you finally establish the necessary feeling of confidence and safety that it takes to ski a fast downhill really aggressively and smoothly.

Highly important when you are afraid is full concentration on perfect balance. A great secret of balance is managing to relax the muscles that are not directly involved in guiding and tracking your skis, such as your hands, arms, shoulders, back, and face. Control your position, but stay as supple as possible at the same time! Always try to keep your arms and hands in front of your low body position.

To ski a perfect DH tuck, get into as low a position as possible. The upper body is parallel to the ground, and you feel your thighs against your chest. If you make yourself as small as possible while standing on a chair in front of a mirror with your ski boots on, you'll easily find the ideal position for yourself. The lower the position you ski, the wider your stance must be with your boots in order to have your skis flat on the snow. Extremists may have their bodies in between their thighs and take a really wide stance for a short distance. As the terrain gets more difficult you have to move into a higher position in order to be more flexible. Immediately you must deliberately adjust your skis to a narrower stance in order to have them flat on the snow. This constant conscious adjustment of the width of your ski track according to the height of your position has simple anatomical and mechanical bases which you should make yourself feel during training.

Have there been any changes in the form of the low downhill position? Yes, I believe we have a further development of the downhill position, which in a way has stagnated ever since the French introduced "la position de l'oeuf," the tuck. Today's world class downhiller skis a slightly different position from that of two or three years ago. Let's take a closer look at it. The real novelty and difference is the new arm position how used by almost all the successful downhillers. In a conventional tuck, you press your poles under your arms and achieve a firm and stable position. With the new downhill tuck, you ski with exactly the same body position, but your hands and arms are holding and pointing the poles freely forward and avoiding any pressing. You may even have to bend your poles slightly, so that they don't get in your way. You should also be determine dto cut the air as far as possible in front of your face by keeping your arms pointed straight forward. To my mind, this new arm position is part of the unusual difference in the gliding results among world class downhillers. Only a racer who has previously practiced this truly uncomfortable position in his physical conditioning program will be able to hold his arms up in the described way under the incredible stresses of a two-minute downhill race and still remain relatively loose. A major advantage of this new arm position is that the connection between the body and thighs is considerably freer, and automatically the racer will absorb small bumps more easily. When you press your poles under your arms , you block this connection and therefore will absorb less friction and will be in the air more, which is naturally slower.

To take a bump at extremely high speed you have to prepare yourself psychologically to face a difficult and dangerous bump calmly. You must accept the following flight, and look at the problem mainly from a technical viewpoint in order to master it well. Better than words are the photo sequences of Herbert Plank, opposite, showing you how you ski a DH bump really well at very high speed.

72

Megève 1975, Downhill. Herbert Plank, Bronze Medal winner at the Olympics, 1976, demonstrates a beautiful tuck with a good arm position at very high speed. Shortly before this picture was taken, the racers jumped a good 60 feet over a road. In 1975 five racers out of the first fifteen fell here. It was the only DH that Franz Klammer did not finish that year, although he was the winner of all the other DH races on the World Cup. Below is Werner Grissman of Austria taking a frightening fall. He did not get hurt.

ABOVE: *Franz Klammer in tuck*

LEFT:
ABOVE: *Rolland Collombin and another racer on the same bump in photomontage.*
BELOW: *Stay low while you're in the air. Franz Klammer and another racer on the same bump in photomontage.*

Generally at extremely high speeds you must approach a drop or a bump in a medium high position and slightly forward. In the following flight you will be subject to great wind friction and will no longer be in touch with the ground, and therefore you must pay great attention to your aerodynamic position while taking this flight. You must concentrate on having the biggest wind catcher, your upper body, relatively parallel to your skis, and you must remain in a low position during the flight. This is very important. Shortly before you land you may stretch out a bit to absorb the landing. If you get stretched out in the air you are in trouble. At very high speeds an erect body catches a lot of wind pressure, and you will get blown backward. Not only do you lose time this way, but you could end up taking a dangerous fall. Therefore, never stretch out immediately after an edge or a bump. The best racers no longer use an extremely deep seat when taking a bump. The reason is that the racers have become faster and faster, and deep seat brings the upper body into an overly erect position, which gets blown backward more easily than torso that is kept parallel to the skis. See the photo of Franz Klammer at page 75.

To sum it all up: The game of th successful downhiller is a combination of great courage joined with many assets: intelligent judgment of his own temporary limits, pleasure in high speeds, a finely developed feeling for eliminating friction wherever it is possible, good technique in high speed curves, a low position over the entire course with the described arm position, the fastest line depending on the conditions (tactics, wax, and so on), confidence to take unexpected flights, an unusual feeling for balance, great willpower, resistance to muscular pains during the race, strong desire to go faster and faster, and a high level of unwavering concentration. This means that only an absolutely fit and well-trained athlete has a chance!

77

Spectators at the Hahnenkamm at Kitzbühel

Conditioning

Physical Conditioning for Ski Racing

Training for your favorite sport must make you happy. You should fill your training sessions with playfulness and enthusiasm, which will have immediate beneficial physical and psychological effects. It is a very good feeling to know that you are fit. While working out hard during physical training sessions, I often imagined ski slopes or next year's races. These daydreams helped me overcome the numerous pains that are symptoms of every really hard workout. The warm shower after a hard training session — what a treat! Only exercises done with the right mental attitude will have the maximum effect on your physical condition.

Nevertheless, training is sometimes all work and pain. Some days you just don't feel like training. Then you should definitely not back out. Train anyway! You should never say, "Today I'm not going, because it is raining," or "Today I am tired, therefore I will not go." Instead you should say, "I might as well get that good feeling of being physically tired after a hard training session." Only concentrated,

Leith running

regular, and good work will help you get in better shape. It is important to learn this at a young age, or else you will have a hard time learning how to be tough on yourself later on.

Here I will describe a way of training which will give you an excellent physical base for your skiing. Today's top racers must continually train their bodies for one of the hardest sports there is. The best national teams have all started to use the time available for their conditioning programs more efficiently. Therefore, they mainly use directly ski-racing-oriented exercises and train mainly the muscle groups that are really involved while skiing. In the following pages I will tell you how to put together a ski-racing-oriented training program similar to the ones the best racers follow. If you are not in top shape you will not win, even if your technique or mental attitude is ready for top performances. If you train according to the following ideas there is no doubt that you will be in top shape next season. But I can only tell you how to train; whether or not you will do it is up to you and your willpower. With your imagination you will be able to create your own individual training program after you have carefully read this part of the book.

What are the Elements of Proper Conditioning?

1. Good overall physical condition
2. Power and force
3. Coordination and courage
4. Flexibility and agility
5. Alert reaction, quickness, and explosiveness
6. Endurance and willpower

These are the areas in which a ski racer should constantly strive for improvement and train for specifically. It is important that you observe yourself. When you feel weak in a particular area — for example, power — you have to train harder in this area than in your specialty — for instance, flexibility, which you are already good at. Always observe yourself carefully, because your body will change, and you will have to adjust your training program according to these body changes. Before you get too bulky from weight-lifting workouts or bicycling, go running and do some flexibility and agility exercises. Training for ski racing is as complex as the sport itself. You need a great deal of variety in your exercises and training sessions.

How Do We Work?

To understand physical training methods you need to understand a few basics about how the body works. Then training will be logical to you. A body that isn't used regularly doesn't get stronger. It becomes fat and weak, and the circulation becomes poor. An untrained body is unable to react quickly under physical stress. Working out regularly is the most important characteristic of a successful training program. When you work with weights, machines, or exercises, you are always using particular muscle groups. Only when you stress a muscle group to at least 70 percent of its total potential will it get a little stronger. If the stress is below 70 percent, there is almost no effect on this muscle or muscle group. You must put a lot of effort and willpower into an exercise to charge your muscle 70 percent, since athletic research shows that an athlete cannot stress a muscle more than 85 to 90 percent of its total potential under normal training or even competitive circumstances. The other 10 to 15 percent reserve represents your natural warning system, great pain or being totally out of breath, which limits your ability to stress yourself more. To surpass 85 to 90 percent of a muscle's potential is possible only for an athlete who feels threatened by fatal danger, and the result is often an injury such as a pulled muscle. The natural warning systems can become distorted by the intake of certain drugs, which can cause an athlete's death. This was demonstrated by Tom Simpson, former world bicycle champion, when he fell off his bicycle dead, in the Tour de France. The thorough investigation of this case showed that he had been using amphetamines. Under normal circumstances it is unknown in the world of sports for a healthy athlete to reach such a high level of exhaustion that he dies. There is no limit on how hard you may try, the harder the more effective.

The methods we use the most are the *interval principle* and the *repetition principle*. First, let's talk about the *interval principle,* the most successful training method invented by the runners. Almost *every* top athlete uses the interval principle when training. Some use it more than others, but it certainly is a very good method. Interval training is used mainly with running. If the interval principle is applied to running and exercises together, in the form of a circuit, you call it *circuit training.* If you apply it to exercises only, it is called the *repetition principle.*

The word *interval* means pause. In other words, you should not exercise constantly, and move around in a "steady state" when you train. In interval training you rhythmically interrupt your hard runs or exercises, each of which you perform with a high standard of quality. If you do your exercises right, you will often reach a level of exhaustion. Depending on the running distances you are using and the number of exercises you decide to do for the day, you may use up to 60 intervals during a one- or two-hour-long session. When you stop after an exercise, immediately measure your pulse rate underneath your chin or on your wrist. Count 10 seconds, and multiply by 6. Your pulse should go up to 180 to 200 beats a minute at the end of an exercise. (Well-trained young athletes reach pulse rates around 220 beats per minute after a really hard performance.) Then wait until your pulse drops to 120 beats per minute, and repeat the particular exercise. This way you can go full out during each exercise without being afraid of hurting or overworking your body. After a while you will develop feeling for when you are ready to go again, and you won't have to measure your pulse each time. Just check your feeling with a watch every once in a while.

When you repeat an exercise while your heart is still beating 130 beats a minute and over, it is too early to do so. You would be too slow and the quality of the exercise wouldn't be good. But don't let your pulse drop below 120 beats per minute before you repeat an exercise again. During the intervals you should deliberately relax yourself. This way, you will recover much more quickly from the high pulse and tiredness in your muscles.

The *interval principle, circuit training,* and the *repetition principle* enable you to train at a higher-quality level for a longer period of time than other training methods, which neglect the immense value of rest and relaxation periods between exercises. Never forget the principle "Tension Needs Relaxation" (see page 121). Try to relax all the muscles not directly involved in performing an exercise or motion. All the sports greats, including Gustavo Thoeni, Muhammad Ali, Jimmy Connors, and Pelé, have this point in common. The use of interval training is something that can support a big step forward in your racing career.

To start a training session you have to loosen up and run for at least 15 or 20 minutes. Run hard enough so that you are sweating slightly. Then you are ready to start your actual training. Also remember to run easily and stretch loosely after each training session before you quit and go in for a shower.

Overall Physical Condition

To get in "good overall physical condition" in order to be able to begin your specific training for ski racing, you have to do a few more things than the average person who just wants to be healthy. The basis for good physical condition is a good cardiovascular system and a well-muscled body. Good health is dependent upon a good way of living and regular sports activities. Some of you don't have well-muscled bodies yet, but you will certainly grow into them while skiing, **83** training, and participating in other sports throughout the year. Running and bicycling are a couple of good exercises to get in generally good shape. For alpine racers, however, these two exercises should not be overdone, particularly not in a long-distance, steady manner. At the beginning of your training in June, you may take one or two bicycle rides or long-distance runs each week for about 45 minutes apiece. When you run, do it in an "elegant" way, with quick small steps when the terrain is hilly, and long loose steps when it is flat and smooth. Watch out for rough terrain, and don't sprain your ankles (particularly those of you who have weak ones). All kinds of sports, such as tennis, soccer, or mountain climbing, are good for your overall condition. They also add a lot of fun to your conditioning program and help develop your competitive playful spirit.

After a few weeks you should be in good enough shape to start using more specifically ski-oriented exercises. Bicycle and run long distances only once every ten days from now on, and only once every two weeks later in the fall. You have to plan your training sessions creatively and individually. Creative imagination is one of the most important parts of your training. Some of you need more power, others more coordination or agility. But remember that all six mentioned elements must be included in your program.

Every once in a while during your hard training sessions have a smile on your face, watch nature. Try to get as much pleasure out of training as possible.

Power and Force

You need power and force to be quick and explosive. In ski racing you need to be quick and explosive in the starting gate, in lateral steps, skating steps, taking a bump in downhill, and making recoveries. Below are exercises which develop more power and force for all the important muscles in ski racing. These skiing-oriented exercises will develop mainly your quadriceps and your midsection (back, stomach,

Here you see a few exercises done by Bernhard Russi while he was training at a Swiss National Team dryland training camp. For all of the exercises that he shows here you should apply the repetition principle. For exercises No. 1 and No. 2 you can also use an isometric form and hold the position for 30–45 seconds with 3–5 repetitions.

Bernhard is one of the finest athletes on the racing circuit. Besides being a brilliant technician, he is in top physical shape. In 1970 he was World Champion in downhill, in 1972, Gold Medal winner in the Olympic downhill at Sapporo, in 1976, Silver Medal winner in Innsbrück.

and sides). Study some of the ski photos and see how important those muscle groups are. You also need strong arms for the start and for your pole plant. But don't do too much for your chest! It wouldn't be helpful to get too heavy or bulky in your upper body.

When you train one particular muscle group you should train the antagonist muscle group as well. A muscle must have a resistance to work against in order to function well. Some years ago the best shot putters and discus and javelin throwers emphasized the development of the actual action muscle. In other words, they trained only the muscles that seemed to do all the work, the pushing and throwing. But new athletes, coaches, and scientists proved them wrong. About ten years ago they started to develop the counter-action muscles with equal care. Today the top athletes all throw 10 percent farther as a result of the improved training methods. If you were to train only one muscle group it would get very big but you could never use its total potential unless you had an antagonist muscle of equal quality. Here I must mention the universal weight machine which is a great help for this kind of training. You can hardly make a mistake using such a machine after a good warm-up. However you certainly don't need a machine, though it takes more imagination and experience to find the right exercises while training hard without mechanical aids. Quickly writing down what you will be doing in a particular session can be a great help. Just get this straight: a training session for "power and force" without suffering isn't worth a damn and it's even better when you enjoy your training, even though it hurts.

With or without weights, you should work with the repetition principle. Remember the wise words of Armin Scheurer, one of the greatest track and field coaches in the world: "Eight to ten repetitions are not enough, two times eight to ten repetitions are still not enough, three times eight to ten repetitions are the right measurement." Then you will really benefit from an exercise. You don't have to train ten different exercises for power in one session; just take four, but do them right. Of course the number of repetitions per exercise varies according to what kind of shape you are in and the stress that is involved in each exercise. You can use anywhere from fifteen to sixty repetitions, total, per exercise. When you train with weights, it would be a great help if you could find a competent coach with experience in working with athletes and weights who could advise you. The proper use of weights is a very individual matter, and using the wrong weights in the wrong way can be more harmful than helpful. When you work out with heavy weights, it's essential to pick up the weight correctly. Bend your knees and pick up the weight with a straight back. Workouts with heavy weights (up to 80 percent of your body weight) are excellent for improving your explosiveness and strength.

From the drawings (page 92) you can see a number of exercises you can choose from. Settle on the muscle groups you want to develop, and use your creative imagination to invent more exercises. Always apply the repetition principle, with three times eight to twelve repetitions. If you make up a circuit training sequence, choose about six of these exercises according to your needs. Repeat each exercise ten times, then rest for a short while before you easily run over to the next exercise. After you've done all six exercises once, take a longer break, resting 2 to 5 minutes or longer, if your pulse isn't down to 120 beats a minute before you repeat the circuit. Do three repetitions.

The following two interval forms are also very good for your power and force.

1. Practice sprints on a smooth fast surface. Sometimes it may go slightly uphill. Choose distances of 30, 40, 50, up to 100 yards at the maximum. Always sprint as fast as possible and keep track of your pulse rate. Repeat the sprints eight to ten times. Train at least three different distances in a 30-minute-interval sprint training. Make sure you warm up sufficiently beforehand.
2. Run along slowly, then start quickly and sprint as fast as you can. When you reach your highest speed, go back to slow running, and try to recover while jogging as relaxed as possible. When you feel rested and ready, start another short sprint. Repeat eight times and rest.

Coordination, Courage, and Balance

Coordination and courage are both very important for a ski racer, and are closely related. Whenever you have a chance to learn a new and difficult exercise take some time to do so. The more difficult motions your body has learned, the easier it will be for you to learn new things or to correct a weakness in your skiing. To train for courage you face a slightly more difficult problem. Since fear and courage are always connected, you have to choose exercises that are slightly dangerous and could hurt you a little bit. However, please avoid any stupid risks like schussing where no one else does. This would result sooner or later in a couple of months in the hospital.

The trampoline and, particularly, the diving board are great facilities for testing your courage. I consider the diving board quite a bit better. First of all, you can practice alone, and second, you can't really hurt yourself beyond a red back and stomach. You need a lot of courage to try a dive you have never done before. Learning new dives also improves your coordination. The trampoline is much more dangerous unless you are working with a group. You should never train by yourself on a trampoline.

Ingemar Stenmark emphasized in several interviews that he considered his specific balance training program a significant factor in his success. He said that he spent up to 15 minutes almost every day on a rope tied between two trees in his back yard. As he got better, he invented all sorts of different exercises like balancing in a low position or on one foot. Now let me list some exercises for your coordination and for your balance.

1. To improve your balance you can walk on fences. When you are so good that it becomes boring, tell your partner to throw you a ball, and try to catch it and throw it back to him. This will make it much more fun and more difficult. Also learn to balance in medium and low positions.

2. While running, cross your feet, then cross your feet forward

and backward while running sideways. Do different types of jump and ballet-type jumps. Run slowly, jump up on one leg, turn 360° in the air, and land softly on the same leg you jumped up with. Repeat a few times and switch legs.

3. Learn how to do forward and backward rolls, one roll after the other, connected smoothly, if possible on grass. Also learn to roll sideways, connect the rolls to make a full circle, change sides.

4. Clap different rythms with your hands and create a jump or an exercise for it.

5. Spend some time doing floor gymnastics, and learn exercises like forward somersaults, handsprings, diving head rolls over objects, with and without the help of a springboard or mini trampoline.

6. Games and sports in which you develop your technique and learn new skills are excellent for improving your coordination.

There are many more exercises you can do for your coordination. Use your imagination. Maybe you can remember an exercise from school. You might try this one. While standing, join your left leg and your right arm to form a circle; your right hand holds your left foot. Now jump through this circle with your right leg, forward and backward, and then switch sides. A little help: at the beginning you may hold on to something with the other arm. Congratulations to those who succeed in doing this exercise. With practice any of you will be able to do it.

Flexibility and Agility

To get into some of the extreme positions demanded by modern technique or to perform a quick recovery, you need to be flexible and

agile. This also helps you ski smoothly and in a supple way, but achieving flexibility and agility takes a lot of regular bending and stretching, which should be done along with the obligatory running at the beginning and end of each training session. When you plan to train with weights or sprints, it is twice as important that you bend and stretch before and afterward. Try to give all your exercises a graceful look and always perform and exercise smoothly with the entire body.

Standing

1. Loosely rotate your arms forward and backward, rising on your toes when your arms are on their way up.
2. Touch the ground with your hands, keeping your legs straight.
3. Rotate your hips, leaning first to one side and then the other.
4. While walking, swing your legs in front of you as high as you can. Start easily and increase the stretching slowly. Keep the swinging leg straight.
5. Walk on your toes, stretch, and reach as high as you can with your hands.
6. Walk in a "tiny position" as close as possible to the ground.
7. Reach backward to touch your left heel with your right hand; reverse sides.
8. Spread your legs and touch your left foot with your right hand; reverse. Make sure you keep your knees straight.

Sitting and Lying

1. Sit on the ground with legs spread out. Touch your left toes with your right hand; reverse. Don't bend your knees.
2. Lie flat on your back. Slowly lift your legs with your knees straight, roll over backward until you can touch the ground with your toes, still keeping your knees straight. Roll forward and touch your head to your knees. Repeat a few times.
3. Lie flat on the ground, either on your back or on your front, with your arms outstretched. Touch your left hand with your right foot; then reverse the exercise.

One of Ingemar Stenmark's favorite exercises, which he does almost daily in the summertime, is balancing. In his backyard he tied a rope between two trees about two feet off the ground.

4. Lie on your stomach and rock back and forth, holding your ankles with your hands.
5. Sit down and spread out your legs for stability. Swing your upper body and arms to the right and to the left. Your eyes should follow your hands.

Use your imagination to create more exercises if you want to. A yoga or gymnastics book might help you. You don't need more than 8 or 10 minutes to stretch and bend your body properly during the warmup. Afterward, you can go on to harder exercises without being afraid of pulling a muscle. If it is really cold you may extend your warmup slightly, both the running and the stretching part. The better shape you are in, the more time you must take for a thorough warmup. In late fall it may extend to 20 minutes, because you are getting in better shape and the weather is getting colder.

Quickness, Explosiveness, and Reaction

Here you will use many of the same exercises you already know from the section "Power and Force." Power and quickness are very closely related. You have to be strong before you can be quick. When you are training particularly for power and force, you always work extremely hard, mostly using the three-times-ten repetition principle until your muscles become tired and begin to ache. The difference between power training and training for quickness is in the number of repetitions and the total time of performance for each exercise. To become quicker and more explosive, you need to train with this particular goal in mind. Don't just repeat each exercise a few times, but do each as explosively as possible. Rest until you really can give everything again.

93

For the following exercises you apply the repetition principle. You can use them individually or in circuits: (1) arms, (2) stomach, (3) torso, (4) back, (5) legs. For the third one at 2, use a medicine ball. For 3 and 4, use a weight of 15-30 pounds, depending on your own capacity. The last one in 5 uses boards set in the ground.

Always use numerous exercises. Try to combine your quickness with smoothness and elegance. One more time: you can achieve quickness only by a maximum effort to be explosive. In October and November you must take time in every training session to improve your quickness, explosiveness, and reaction time. Use the exercises below plus the ones from the section "Power and Force."

1. Run sprints of 30 yards up to a maximum of 100 yards. Sprint down a slight hill.

2. Perform a few fast knee bends (about three times five repetitions). You should normally use weights of between 50 and 80 pounds, but for fast deep knee bends use a weight of 20 pounds only.

3. Do stretch jumps, lateral jumps, and 360° jumps on one leg. Perform only a few of each jump, but at their highest quality.

4. Do pushups, jackknives, diving head rolls, handsprings, somersaults, and other gymnastics and exercises.

5. A two-man soccer game with one partner as the goalie and the other partner trying to score as many goals as possible is great for your quickness and reactions. Switch roles.

6. Last, but not least, there is wood slalom. Wood slaloms were always an important element in an alpine racer's training and still are. You should add them to your training at least once every week starting in September. However, it is better to use slalom poles than the trees in the forest. Use slightly falling terrain and not a mountain. The course should have 15 to 20 gates, and you should sprint through them with small steps as fast as you can. You will find yourself performing ski positions automatically. This is a good way to start working on additions to your technique and on correcting old mistakes. It is especially good for working on your pole plant, arm position, a square upper body, and the principle "Tension Needs Relaxation." Repeat the course a few times, and always rest enough between runs.

Most of these exercises are extremely skiing-oriented. You will get muscles where you really need them. You will be able to perform miracles on the course, and make recoveries quickly. Regular hard work is the key!

Endurance, Stamina, and Willpower

Regular hard workouts, including training specifically for power and quickness, will have a favorable influence on your willpower and endurance. But every once in a while you must train particularly for endurance. Long-distance running and bicycling are two good exercises, but don't do them too often. You have to train for the type of endurance and willpower that is involved in ski racing. This is the ability to give everything within two minutes. You must learn to get yourself together even when pain and exhaustion are almost killing you at the end of a long downhill or giant slalom.

Very good ways to learn this kind of stamina, endurance, and willpower are interval sprints and fast runs over distances of 220 yards with eight repetitions and 440 yards with six repetitions, but not during the same training session. To my mind, longer distances are not particularly good for alpine ski racing, at least in interval form. Even though an interval run of 440 yards takes barely 1 minute, the training effect of six 440-yard intervals is quite enough to develop endurance and stamina for a 2 to 3 minute ski race. If you chose a longer distance, your performance would suffer, and you would develop too slow a pace. Runners, too, always train shorter distances in interval form than those in which they actually will compete. Another good exercise for the type of endurance you need: while running on a field or path, suddenly start sprinting for 200 yards, and then recover by jogging. Before you feel quite ready do another sprint, repeat five times. This is an exercise which you should do only when you already feel in pretty good shape. In September you should start to develop endurance and stamina for staying in your tuck. You should do three 3-minute intervals in front of a mirror making sure you have good form. Work on the new arm position! Leap into the air as high as you can, landing softly in your tuck just as you would over a big bump. Try to be fairly relaxed in spite of its being an uncomfortable and stressful position.

As you see, endurance, stamina, and willpower for the alpine ski racer have a very different character than for the long-distance runner or the oarsman. In your endurance training for ski racing you should not get into a "steady state" far below your limits. You must learn how to suffer and often go into an oxygen debt while training. Always combine your endurance training with a relatively high-quality performance.

Recovering from an Injury

All physical sports contain a high risk of injury. Skiing, particularly ski racing, is one of the most dangerous sports there is. Insurance companies in the alpine nations all have higher rates for ski racers. Although many injuries result from unstable personal attitudes, it would be foolish to say that all ski accidents have psychological causes. The cause of an injury may be pure bad luck, a lack of experience in judging dangerous situations, a mistake in setting your bindings, or poor physical condition. On the other hand, there are racers who have psychological tendencies that lead them into accidents. I will talk about some of these psychological problems and tendencies in the section "Injury-prone Athletes" in the chapter "The Racer's Mind." When an athlete is hurt, regardless of the reasons, he or she is confronted with the major problem of how to recover physically.

What should you do if you are injured and truly desire to make it back in ski racing? What follows is my personal advice to the hurt ones among you. Unfortunately, I have had my share of personal experiences in this field. To start with, I must remind you that it takes willpower, patience, and dedication to completely recover from a bad accident. In connection with this section it would help to read about willpower in the chapter "The Racer's Mind." In order to have real willpower you must know and have worthwhile goals. You must dream about the joy you will have when you ski again, and about how beautiful it feels to run through the forest! You must see your total recovery in connection with the overall quality of your life. You need this good motivation in coping with the frustrating beginnings of recovering after a bad accident.

Fausto Radici, Italian Ski Team. As a young child, he lost his right eye. Despite this immense handicap, he belongs to the world class establishment and won a World Cup Slalom in 1976. He is amazing. Notice how he centers his eye, as well as how he skis!

I remember a time when I could barely walk and took my bike out for the first time. After riding ten minutes I was totally out of breath and dizzy, and I felt so weak that I had to quit. But it was a beginning. The next day I rode for 15 minutes and slowly worked my way up. Many people regarded my efforts as insane and gave me no likelihood of recovering completely. I was down to 110 pounds and had 22 screws and two plates in my leg, but my doctor, who had performed a miracle with a bone transplant and by fixing my badly broken knee joint, always encouraged me to give it a full-out try. When I mentioned my ambition to race again professionally, he said, "Sure, why not?" His support meant a lot to me. After three full years of absence from ski racing, I raced again on the ISRA pro circuit. I was in better shape than ever before in my life and had a fantastic time racing that year. Not only did I recover fully from my accident, but I also repaired my self-esteem, which was badly damaged after the accident. The three years between my accident and my first race were filled with thousands of sacrifices and extremely regular training, which wasn't always fun. But it was also one of the most beautiful times in my life. You can hardly imagine how deeply happy and appreciative I felt when I was finally able to run again in the forest, and when I could finally make a few decent turns again in powder. The greatest reward of all was when I won my first race again, the elimination race of the ISRA season opener at Vail, Colorado. It was worth all my efforts and the three years I had dedicated fully to my body and beloved sport.

The most helpful factors in my recovery were the training methods I learned while working on my physical education degree at the Swiss Federal Sports School. Regularity and a high level of intensity in your training are the keys to total recovery. It is impossible to give you a specific outline on how to recover from a bad injury. Only an extremely individual training program adjusted particularly to your injury will result in success. I strongly advise you to seek professional help when you outline your recovery program. I must mention the fact that a well-educated physical education teacher, a football coach, a physiotherapist, or a specialist in sports medicine may be able to give you better advice than many doctors. A surgeon is often not familiar

99

with the latest training methods in sports and knows little about specific exercises and their training effects. Many doctors won't agree with this statement, but most experienced athletes and coaches have found my observations to be true.

What else can you do to help yourself recover? First of all, you must keep track of your progress with a scale and measuring tape. It is a great motivation to see yourself gaining back muscle and weight, and it is also an accurate indicator of how strong you are. You must also watch carefully that you don't favor your injured leg or other injured body part in daily life when you're walking or standing around. You must realize that the temporary atrophy of your injured leg must be taken seriously, and that the earlier you start rebuilding your muscles, the better chance you have to recover fully. Laziness or simply lack of knowledge could change a temporary atrophy into a permanent one.

You shouldn't start putting extreme amounts of stress onto your injured leg by very heavy training until the measuring tape shows that your legs are equally strong again. It is of utmost importance that your injury is completely recovered and that both legs (or arms, shoulders, or whatever) are equally strong before you start running gates or even free-skiing hard. If you go skiing too early, not only will you run a big risk of reinjuring yourself, but you will also favor your injured leg. As a result, you will be slow and may well cause a further atrophy of your injured leg. Ski racing is not a sport in which you become good overnight. An additional two-month delay won't spoil your chances to make it, and afterward you'll be ready to ski really well again with two equally strong legs. Two months of poor technical skiing when you are not ready could be disastrous for your body and your way of skiing.

Below are some specific exercises for common ski injuries:

After a broken leg, or a knee injury, your thigh and your quadriceps are usually your weakest muscles. When building your thigh back up, you must exercise the antagonist of each muscle you want to get stronger. For example, you must build up both your quadriceps and hamstrings in order to gain your full strength back. This principle is explained in more detail in the section "Power and Force."

There are four major muscle groups in your thigh that must be exercised: the quadriceps, the hamstrings, the sartorius, and the rectus femoris. See the stick figures on page 92 for exercises for the quadriceps and the hamstrings. The sartorius and the rectus femoris are the muscle groups on the inside and outside of your thigh. To exercise them efficiently, get an old bicycle inner tube. Attach the inner tube to the leg of a heavy couch and put your foot through the other end. Now pull your leg slowly as far as you can to the left and right while sitting on the floor. Increase the repetitions from fifteen to thirty times on both sides. Use the repetition principle. After you feel in pretty good shape, you may take up bicycling. Only when your legs are pretty equal in strength is it advisable to take up running.

To build up weak ankles or to recover from a sprained ankle you should do toe raises. You may work up to pretty heavy weights or use a partner. A good method of gaining strength quickly is to do three intervals of toe raises, and each time keep on going until you just can't continue any longer. Jumping rope is also a good exercise for weak ankles. Isometric exercises where you push up, down, toward the outside and then the inside with your foot are also good. Watch out that you don't sprain your ankle again in dry-land training. People with weak ankles should not run on rough terrain.

A typical ski injury is a dislocated shoulder. Some racers' shoulders pop out all the time. It's a nasty injury, but there is a good way to take care of it. You simply circle a weight very slowly and carefully over and around your head fifteen times on each side, and repeat this procedure three times. Start with a light weight and work up to a twenty- or thirty-pound weight. This will take care of almost all bad shoulders if you practice regularly once or twice a day for about a month.

It takes creativity and professional advice to discover exactly the right exercises for each injury. But by studying and learning more and more about your body you will be able to find the right ones. Don't hesitate to find the right professional help even if you have to go out of your way.

A Suggestion for a Training Program

You will get in fantastic shape if you train as hard as I advise you to in the following training program, adjusting it to your individual needs. Remember always: To work out regularly for 45 minutes a day is certainly more beneficial to you than one mammoth 8-hour session a week.

June/July

In this period you have to get in overall good shape, so you can take up hard specific training at the beginning of August. Running and bicycling, two sessions a week for about 45 to 60 minutes, plus other sports.

August

Start of the specifically skiing-oriented exercise program. Three sessions a week for 45 to 60 minutes, plus other sports, one long-distance run every two weeks for at least 45 minutes.

September

Four to five sessions a week, 45 to 90 minutes, plus other sports. Now use the entire set of exercises. Train particularly the middle distances: 220 yards, 440 yards in interval form.

October

Four to five sessions a week, 45 to 90 minutes. Use the entire set of exercises. Train particularly the short distances, up to 100 yards, with the interval principle plus a lot of power and force. Run wood slaloms at least once every week.

November

Every day 30 to 60 minutes, but now on a much higher intensity level. Concentrate on explosiveness, smoothness, and elegance. Warm up a long time and train very hard.

It is important that you keep track of what you do every day by writing a training booklet. In this way, you can improve your personal program from year to year. It is a lot of fun to try to break the training records you set the previous year! For example:

September 28

15 min. warm-up, gymnastics and power exercises, sprints, 10 x 60 yards, plus jumprope, 50 minutes.

September 29

45 min. long-distance run, some work with 30-pound weight, tennis, plus swimming and diving, 2 hours.

October 1

Warmup with coordination exercises, six 440-yard intervals, school soccer, gymnastics, 90 minutes. . . .

How to Keep Fit during the Racing Season

It is important that you keep working out during the entire racing season, not for long periods, but regularly and with emphasis on quality. Make sure that you always wear a scarf and warm clothes if

Good-quality stretch jumps. Form as in skiing. Form a right angle and stay in this position for two minutes. Fix your legs and sink slowly onto your stomach. Great for hamstrings!

you train outside. In addition you should do a daily warmup in the morning before skiing.

The reason for mentioning the exercises below separately is that they are excellent exercises to do indoors during the winter when racing. Please also include them in your fall program along with your workouts for power and force. All three exercises are directly skiing-related. Apply the repetition principle.

Also do lateral jumps regularly. Jumping rope is a good way to keep your cardiovascular system in shape when it's too icy and snowy to run outside. In the winter you must maintain your condition. For this reason I strongly advise you to establish a routine training of 25 to 30 minutes about *two times a week* during the racing season. Train your whole body, but in a more playful way and with fewer repetitions per exercise.

Very hard free skiing in which your muscles really get tired is also an excellent way to keep in shape during the winter.

Test Sheet

Test yourself on the following exercises exactly and properly with **104** the help of your coach or a partner. The first test takes place at the beginning of your training, and the second shortly before the season starts. Compare results from year to year and work on your weaknesses. Watch the quality of your exercises!

1. How many push-ups can you do with clapping your hands? No resting in between push-ups.
2. How many pull-ups can you do?
3. Have someone hold your feet. Hold your hands behind your neck. How many sit-ups can you do in one minute without pausing?
4. Lie on your stomach and throw a medicine ball over a bench against a wall. How many throws can you do in one minute?
5. How many times can you jump rope in two minutes?
6. What is your jumping capacity?
   (a) Stand beside a wall and reach up with your hand. Measure where the top of your fingers touch.
   (b) Jump as high as you can, touching the top with your hand. Measure again. The difference equals your jumping capacity.
7. How flexible are you? Stand on a table and measure how low you can reach with straight legs.
8. How fast can you sprint 60 yards?
9. How fast can you run 440 yards? This is preferably done on an official track.

This test is also a very good training session in itself. Before you do the test make sure you warm up sufficiently just as you do before any hard training session.

Final Training Advice

Now you know enough to create a thorough physical training program for yourself. No one can help you more than yourself. Use your imagination sensibly and creatively. Remember that quality is more important than quantity. Work regularly, train intensively, give a **105** lot, and go through some real pain every so often. Learn how to relax totally and recover quickly. Vary your training, and you won't get bored. If you want to become a good racer, training has to come first.

Live in a healthy way, and keep away from smoking, drinking, and other drugs. It is important in the long run. I will discuss this more in the section "Emotions in Ski Racing." Food and the way you eat are also important. It's odd but true that athletes often start crash diets at the same time that they take up training. They want to do everything at once. Of course it doesn't work this way. When you train hard you need a lot of energy, because you usually get very hungry. It is a fact that eating starches after a hard training session has a positive influence on a quick recovery. You don't have to worry about getting fat after a hard training session even when you eat a bowl of spaghetti. Eating a lot of meat and other protein foods such as cheese, nuts, milk, yogurt, and soybeans is essential if you want to have the maximum results from your power and force training. Proteins are the building blocks used to strengthen a muscle. Make sure you eat good-quality food. Appreciate and enjoy your meals; chew well and slowly. Don't get lost in the confectionary shops when racing in Europe for the first time. There are many fine books about nutrition, and it would be worth your while to educate yourself a little more about nutrition.

But now I have to mention a problem which will come up when you first start skiing again. You will have gained a lot of new muscle if you trained properly. You may feel quite funny the first few days on skis again, because your body is so strong and your new muscles aren't used to the very complicated motions in ski racing yet. Don't worry when this happens to you. It will be a matter of a few days until your muscles have fully adapted, and then you will ski better than ever before in your life.

If you think that my recommendations on physical training are too demanding, you are definitely mistaken. I have observed the training programs of the Swiss, the Austrians, the French, and the Italians for many years. They are all very strongly oriented toward outstanding physical condition for each team member.

I must remind you that this book doesn't train you. These are only words. Now it is up to you to put the words into action and set up your own training program.

The Racer's Mind

Introduction

During my years at the Swiss Federal School of Physical Education at Magglingen, I wrote an essay on the psychology of competitive sports for my teacher Urs Weber, who was also director of the Swiss Alpine Ski Team at that time. From those days on, I have remained interested in the questions that challenged my mind when I wrote that paper.

It's definitely necessary to take a look at the values of today's sports world, which are very questionable. Some are truly disgraceful. Today we are confronted with an extremely materialistic sports world directed by big companies. Whether this is good or bad is not the question here, but it has had a negative impact on many sportsmen in the last two decades, including some very "successful" athletes.

Not too long ago the word *sport* was linked with the word *hobby*. That's the way I've always felt and still do feel about our sport of ski racing, although I became a professional and enjoy the competitive side of the sport as well. In the following sections I will talk about important influences and factors in the "racer's mind." Everyone is different.

109

Why Racing? Impulses and Motives

For anything we do professionally or as a sport or hobby, we need an impulse: good or bad, well-founded or not, spiritual or financial. Whether or not an impulse is a good one, we learn from the psychological results. Not everyone with good and proper motivations becomes successful or a world champion as a consequence, but if you have healthy impulses and motivations you will reach a higher personal standard than if you don't. Good motivation is sort of like a puzzle. You have to fit the parts of your motivation puzzle together when you really decide to ski race and create a future for yourself which you can look forward to, not one which is frightening to you. You must see great things in it for you.

You can only reach your goal of becoming a top ski racer over the long term. When you are a very good junior racer it will still take you a minimum of half a dozen years to become a really top racer. And the way there is a rocky hard road. You have to overcome streaks of bad performances, setbacks, and sometimes even injuries. To feel a solid inner call and a great love for your sport is absolutely necessary if you want to become a top ski racer. Because of the immense stress situations an alpine racer faces while following the circuit, such as travel, weather, fear, risks, and changes in emotions, I consider alpine ski racing one of the toughest sports around.

Someone who is just a great physical talent no longer wins races nowadays. You have to combine a whole package of different qualities to be a top racer, and you must develop these qualities as a young junior. If you truly love your sport, a lot of things will automatically fall into place. You must establish a long-term friendship with skiing and give yourself some time to become good. No one becomes a good flutist or piano player in two years even if he has the greatest talent and the best instruction. It's a puzzle that has to fit together and relax you, instead of putting pressure on you, combining love for motion, idealism, physical and mental joy in your performances, a special love for being outdoors, ambition, a love for competition, and sure knowledge of your plans beyond ski racing.

This sequence shows Rosi Mittermaier in Olympic slalom 76, which she won. She was a double Gold Medal winner at the 1976 Olympics in downhill and slalom, also won a Silver Medal in the Olympic giant slalom, and the World Cup Championship in combined and in slalom. Rosi is one of the most amazing people in ski racing. She has been on the German ski team for over ten years. Two to three times she had to change her technique drastically to stay at the top. She even became a great downhiller toward the end of her career.

Rosi, the 25-year-old lady from Germany, was certainly the racer with the most experience on the World Cup circuit. She had belonged to the world class establishment of the "top ten" for almost a decade. Then she finally won overwhelmingly. Rosi is very well liked by the other girls on her team, who called her "Mom" during her last years of racing.

One wonders whether some ski administrators and politicians aren't sometimes a little quick in their decision to drop an older athlete from the team just because he or she has to overcome a crisis, an accident or a change in technique.

The performances of today's top ski racers are widely used by the manufacturers in their advertising. They try to make people believe that the product wins and not the racer himself, or, at least, that he is just a part of it. After the 1974 world championships, Switzerland's largest newspaper reported that slow skis were responsible for the defeat of their best downhillers and thereby damaged the reputation of one of the top ski manufacturers.

Some years ago, the best racers became aware of their actual value and started working out contracts with the manufacturers regardless of their "amateur" status. Indeed Bob Beattie's pro circuit seemed to me to have had more amateurs during its first years than the F.I.S. amateur circuit. The only difference between the two circuits was that the top amateurs made more money and declared less. Many racers who were top "amateurs" during the early '70s would have made less money if they had turned professional. To be fair, the Americans were the exception. The racers on the U.S. Ski Team were the last true amateurs on the World Cup circuit, but they weren't winning. Many became worried about their futures before they reached their peaks. As amateurs they had a full-time job but didn't get paid for it. Consequently the best ones steadily turned pro to make a living. Now matters appear to look a little different.

This short description of the commercial involvement of the top racers may explain the greedy and unhealthy money-oriented attitudes and motivations of some of the best racers and of some younger racers aiming for the same return. Indeed, I know "amateur" racers who sold their chances to win an Olympic medal on the green table. They signed contracts with manufacturers of an obviously inferior product rather than skiing on the equipment they really liked but which paid less. They knew it and accepted their defeat with a greedy smile. They were businessmen, and obviously their performance was less important to them than money. Bad results automatically followed their decision. They never found out what ski racing really could have given them.

Why do I mention these rather sad and unpleasant examples? Simply because I think these temptations are very hard to avoid for almost every up-and-coming talent. Sooner or later you will be confronted with these problems as you approach the top. Commercialism is a dangerous factor in ski racing. Watch out, young racer! A "good contract" is not a permanent existence and is surely no education for later life. Please get your head straight on this point. I don't say that an extremely commercially motivated athlete has no chance. There are plenty of racers around who have proved the contrary. However, I'm sure the more idealistic athlete has a better time and is happier. He will also continue to enjoy sports for the rest of his life even after his career is over.

Some people with completely result-oriented values have a tough influence on the young talented racer. Parents, and totalitarian coaches doing everything for a salary, provide fully ski-oriented programs for their kids. They want their kids to make it on their terms. I don't think that this is a very healthy procedure for most kids. At the age of fourteen or fifteen they have been manipulated in one direction, and for many it will be a frustrating experience, since they also have talents elsewhere. Think of this no matter how good you are: have time for other things besides ski racing and then accept a long-term apprenticeship to get to the top, if you truly love it and want to be good at it. Take the pressure off your skiing career by leaving other doors open and caring about your education. A famous long-distance runner once said, "The best way to set a new record is to give yourself time for doing it." I'm sure he meant the years of regular training. This is true for alpine racing too. The willpower and long-distance goal of the older athlete may win in the end.

Willpower is a very complex human quality and depends a great deal on your motivations, ego, and ambitions. You must clearly realize that desire and willpower are not dependent on physical power and technical skills, although you need both to apply your willpower to training and racing. The ultimate rule is: You must know the goal you want to reach. Failures in willpower are caused by not knowing exactly what you want and how to achieve it. A solid knowledge of technique and physical conditioning methods combined with an appropriate goal are necessary in order for you to be able to use all the willpower you have available. The young impatient racer often reaches too high. Failure to reach his goal damages his athletic self-esteem and takes the joy out of his sport. Be very careful when setting yourself goals. Make achievements step by step. Every once in a while you may have a really hard goal, but it has to lie within the realistic reach of your abilities.

Besides willpower, mental and physical endurance and a certain stubbornness are qualities in a racer's character. They help you over-come the bad breaks and the downs that are included in any sports career. A good ski racer must develop good self-confidence and self-reliance, but, most of all, he must keep his humility. It's important that you don't mix up self-confidence and arrogance. An arrogant state of mind limits your creative conception and learning capacity to a minimum and has a bad effect on team spirit as well. It can also lead to grave accidents if an arrogant young racer refuses to accept his limits. This has finished more than one ski racing career.

Emotions in Ski Racing

The noblest commandment is to love your sport and to train with idealism. If you basically feel this strongly about skiing, you will be a happy sportsman no matter what your overall achievements are. If you truly love ski racing, it will be easier for you to accept and take the ups and downs, victory and defeat, without overvaluing either of them. You will also be ready to expend some of your younger years without hunting for materialistic goals. When you acquire material luxuries in later years, you will realize that they alone don't provide happiness.

Every true ski racer knows the incredible rewards you get when overcoming "hairy" situations with the help of your courage on a fast downhill or when free skiing on a difficult mountain, using all your skills and imagination. That's happiness too! A sport like ski racing

requires a lot of love and idealism to meet all the sacrifices you will have to make for it, since the apprenticeship is a long one. Becoming a recognized racer on the national level takes a great amount of intensive practice and training. Furthermore, to be one of the hundred best ski racers in the world just doesn't lie within most young athletes' grasp. But merely reaching a high level of achievement is not all ski racing can give you back for your hard training. If you really give it a hard try and work with enthusiasm, ski racing will bring out and develop important human qualities, such as endurance, willpower, physical and mental toughness, courage, the ability to change and learn, concentration, self-confidence, and humility. On the other hand, sports may also influence in a negative way basic human faults such as vanity, overaggression, false pride, conceit, narrow-mindedness, insecurity, and asocial behavior.

Never forget that sports represent playing as well as plain competition. Playing is one of the main occupations and privileges of men. Unlike animals, human beings enjoy playing at all ages, while older animals are a lot less playful than younger ones. Only human beings constantly keep developing until very old age, driven by their intelligence, spirit, and emotions.

Emotional stress comes in all sorts of forms. It may arise through personal differences with your teammates or coaches. With goodwill on both sides, these usually can be worked out. Sometimes you will be lonely, and the different customs you come across while traveling to the races may irritate rather than excite you. The first time you ski in front of a big audience you may tense up. Instead of having your mind on yourself, you may chat with or think about the spectators and consequently lose your concentration. In the section "Slalom" I mentioned that a top racer must have a certain amount of easy-goingness. Only this way can you take the calculated risks and chances necessary to place well when the pressure is really on.

Another dangerous source of emotional stress is the press. The sensational newspapers in all countries often play a particularly bad role this way. I know of a world class racer who sold his exclusive interview for a relatively high sum to a sensational paper before the world championships in Portillo, Chile. Under this extra stress caused by an eager journalist, this particular athlete skied way below his ability. During the last few years I've watched a number of top racers announce in the press their plans to win the World Cup, a race, or a medal. Almost none of them succeeded! In most cases, such statements worked against these athletes. They simply put pressure on themselves, and winning became an obligation to them. They should have known that there is nothing more enjoyable than a good surprise. Sometimes a young racer may get caught in this circle without being fully aware of it, and suddenly he or she is pressured into the hard role of a favorite. To keep your highest goal as your own secret is not a bad idea.

Sports on the top level have created many victims, particularly when the individuals involved don't see any other way to fulfill themselves except by being successful in their sport. They looked at their sport in a completely totalitarian way. Not too long ago, there was an Austrian racer who committed suicide a few weeks after his disastrous performance (for an Austrian) at the world championships in 1970. Newspapers put him down and close associates turned their backs on him, and he just couldn't take it anymore. He was a sensitive young man completely channeled into becoming a ski racer. His world fell in on him when he failed to race well in the world championships. Unfortunately, his example doesn't stand alone; similar incidents have happened in all sports. I know of several other top racers who quit ski racing because of nervous breakdowns. This is why it is so important to justify your goals and seek for the best values in your sport on a broad basis.

What happens when you are winning, when you become a great champion, when you have a streak of victories? Being a champion or a winner has its own problems. If you ever are a winner, try to be a good one, keep your humility, stay modest, and be a good example for the young ones. Celebrating a great performance or victory is of great importance. When Tina Illiffe won the downhill at Courchevel, France, in 1973 we had plenty of reason to celebrate. It was the first British victory in a major European international ski race in thirty-six years. Despite the heavy economic crises that had hit England at that time, the manager of the team, Mrs. Maria Goldberger, ordered a couple of bottles of fine French champagne with dinner. We had a hell of a time, and I am happy to recall that each team member enjoyed that evening.

However, there is a great difference between celebrating and getting drunk. Alcohol is a drug and not a harmless one. It's the drug that is the most accepted and integrated in our society. But in the last decade other drugs have had a great influence on the youth in the U.S.A. and Western Europe, such as marijuana, hashish, cocaine, hallucinogens, and amphetamines. Some athletes may want to improve their performances through drugs. Others use drugs for emotional stimulation and support, or for social acceptance. But we have to make two points clear: drugs can be dangerous, and they are all around us. An athlete who is a regular user of marijuana or alcohol usually takes care of himself. Sooner or later he will drop out of racing. However, there were and are athletes who have used marijuana occasionally and have gotten drunk sometimes, yet still achieved top results in sports. Even though many athletes frankly admit to you in a private conversation that they occasionally use alcohol or marijuana, it certainly doesn't represent a major part of their life-style. A regular user of either drug, not to mention the heavier ones, will go down the drain faster than he thinks.

For some reason it seems to be harder for American kids to deal with drugs. When I first arrived in the United States I was only nineteen. I went to a bar and ordered a beer. "Where is your ID?" asked the bartender. I had to order a Coke, but it didn't bother me any further. Since I was a young European, wine and beer were nothing special to me, and I didn't expect any particular high from drinking. Apparently American kids do, but it's not their mistake. They are taught by their parents, teachers, drug programs, and society in general to expect a high from alcohol. No wonder it's such a great temptation for young people to want to experience this and other "highs" they are warned about by the adult user.

In conclusion I offer you the following advice. Live in a healthy way, and keep away from smoking and drinking. It is important in the long run. Don't get lost with drugs. Some of you may have experienced drugs and think that you know how to handle them. That's the most important point: that you know how to handle drugs sensibly and in a healthy way without harming you or your sports career. Others may be confused about drugs. Be smart and learn from mistakes others have made, even when they don't admit them. I personally believe that it shouldn't be a big problem for a ski racer who loves his sport and wants to be good in it. In general, you find out quickly how bad it is to get drunk the day before a race or to go out for a conditioning session while stoned. However, many a racer loves to appear as a wild rebellious character and often only learns through bad results. There is nothing against a good party after you've won a race or when you have time for a relaxing break. Draw your own conclusions. Finally it's just you who can make up your mind on how to approach this very touchy subject.

A personal relationship with someone of the opposite sex naturally has a great influence on your emotions. It can be a very good one, and in most cases it is. Athletes are no different from other people. They all have their different sexual needs. Particularly after a race is over and the pressure is gone, athletes are known to develop quite a sexual appetite, and seek this form of communication and relaxation. They are also healthy young human beings who are at the perfect age to fall in love. However, at this point a good coach must remind his athlete of his duties if it seems as if the athlete might get carried away by a romance at the wrong moment: for example, during the days before an important race. This happened to a friend of mine at the 1968 Olympics. At that time, he was one of the world's best GS skiers. The romance only lasted a week, but he raced far below his potential in the Olympic GS. I have to think that he missed out on his sleep.

For a number of years the leading sports authorities insisted that sex was bad for athletes. This is untrue. Too many great athletes report having regular and happy sex lives and many are married. In fact, there are cases where an athlete's performance suffers considerably by being away from his or her lover, friend, wife, or husband.

118

Heini Hemmi of Switzerland winning the Olympic Gold Medal in 1976 in the giant slalom.

Heini is a great skier, although he is not a spectacular one. His aim is to ski very efficiently. Most of the time he is perfectly balanced over the center of his skis and he has an unusually fine feeling for his edges. At 27, he is a veteran on the Swiss team, married and living a regular life. He has been given a long time to peak, but the patience paid off.

Heini is only 5 feet 4 inches tall, and even though he was accepted as being a top giant slalom specialist for years, very few believed he would ever have a big win. But he came out better than Gustavo and Ingemar in the Olympic giant slalom. He overcame his handicap of being smaller than all the other top racers and confirmed his initial success with victories in a couple of giant slalom meets after the Olympics.

Relaxation, Concentration, Yoga

Every experienced sportsman knows how emotions and his temperamental reactions can influence a performance negatively. Therefore it is of great importance that you find a good, stable rhythm in your daily life. When looking at the schedule of an alpine ski racer, you immediately realize how immense the stress is on these athletes who rush from place to place in order to make the next race. The competition is tough, and the constant battle for F.I.S. or World Cup points is another disturbing factor on your mind. The never-ending excitement and the changes in environment are hard on your nerves. You can easily lose your rhythm and suddenly find that you can't sleep, are constipated, tense, and in the end can't ski as you normally do. To avoid these problems it's absolutely necessary that you learn to relax daily and consciously. Jean-Claude Killy said in an interview with *Sport* in Zurich during January 1967, "To relax is most important. The competition is so tough on you mentally and physically that you

Ingemar Stenmark, 1976 World Cup winner and Bronze Medalist in the Olympic giant slalom 1976.

This sequence shows Ingemar in his second giant slalom run in the Olympics. He was well behind the leaders after his first run and only a fantastic second run could reward him with a medal. Well, what else is there to say but "He did it!" Notice Ingemar's great pole plant in this steep icy giant slalom.

should use every minute available to sleep, relax, or for recreation. . . . My life during the season consists of sleeping, eating, and racing." It sounds somewhat boring, but he was plentifully rewarded for his dedication.

Recently hundreds of different methods have been propounded to help human beings relax and find the path to "happiness." Most of the theories are in one way or another related to the ancient Hindu practice of yoga. But yoga in its true sense takes many hours a day. There is no way a top racer can involve himself with this kind of practice.

A few years ago the top national teams started to experiment with yoga-related methods, which led to surprisingly positive results with many athletes. The Swiss team has used a method called autogenic training for many years. Conscious relaxation, yoga, autogenic training, or a combination of these methods can truly help an athlete to relax, concentrate, and level his self-esteem. It can even prevent disease and sickness to an extent. The success of conscious relaxation is dependent on the willingness of the individual athlete to get into these matters by himself.

Success also depends on your capability to practice relaxation when others may be tense, for instance while traveling on a plane, train, or bus. "How do you relax between races?" Annemarie Moser-Proell was questioned by *Ski Racing.* "I sleep," was her answer. The principle "tension needs relaxation" is surely one of the most important in sports, mentally as well as physically. Above all, it seems to me of importance to leave relaxation methods up to the individual. It is good to know how one can relax more efficiently, but to be forced to do it would only create tension.

Autogenic training, which I have used for may years, is a method which helps you relax your mind and body. It is a combination of the Hatha Yoga courses I took in Zurich and Dr. J. H. Schulz's original autogenic training. To begin with you must find a nice, preferably private, corner which you like. There you spread out a blanket and lie down on it. It is essential that you feel in tune with the place where you relax. After lying down on your blanket, close your eyes, relax, and

122

start to breathe regularly, slowly, and deeply. Try to get into a positive state of mind by picturing beautiful happenings. Let every part of your body get really heavy. Concentrate on your little finger until it feels like lead. Next concentrate on relaxing your second finger, and gradually repeat this procedure for each part of your entire body. Completely relax and keep breathing deeply and slowly. After a while, you may fall into a solid sleep, particularly if you are already tired.

If you feel like spending some more time for your conscious relaxation, try this: after you feel really relaxed, tighten all your muscles with a sudden effort as much as you can. At the same time hold your breath. Hold this position for quite a while. Then release the tension in your muscles, breathe deeply, and relax again. Repeat this procedure several times until you feel totally relaxed. As Professor Franz Hoppichler, former Austrian coach, said in an interview concerning the life-style of today's racers, "The more intensively you live the more you need to relax. Otherwise you are tense even when you don't want to be!" If your schedule is tight there is nothing better for you than to use some kind of conscious relaxation. Then you'll be able to cope with the stress more easily.

A relaxed athlete is able to concentrate much better and, most of all, more precisely. You can't concentrate on everything, you have to concentrate on the right things. Here is where a good coach, who knows his athletes well, can do a lot of good by giving clear and precise advice to his racers at the start of a race.

Let us hear what Bobby Cochran has to say about this point: "I don't know how you can define concentration. You have to concentrate on the right things. When a racer makes a mistake people say, 'He lost his concentration!' I don't think that's right. Just think, maybe he wasn't concentrating on the right thing. You can't concentrate on the crowd, on the racer that just went down in front of you who looked pretty fast. You can't concentrate on how you're going to place in the race. . . ." He is right; you can't.

It is your skiing you have to concentrate on, your tactics, and the special little things that you know will gain time. Not only must you concentrate on the right things; you must concentrate on the right

thing at the right time. You shouldn't concentrate on the icy fifth gate when you are starting, or on the mistake you made three gates ago. Concentrate on what's happening and what is coming up immediately in front of you. Maximum physical effort combined with maximum concentration is often necessary to master a particularly difficult section.

As you know by now, a high level of tension and concentration is possible only with adequate relaxation. Physically, you must find short moments of relaxation, even between turns. Your concentration is the one thing you can't let up on during the race. You may concentrate more on one point at a certain time than another, but you have to be with it all the time. Each individual racer must find his own race routine, which is adjusted to his own personality, therefore the following suggestions represent only my particular conclusion. Because you have to concentrate on a high level for the entire time you are on the course, you must give your mind a deliberate rest and relaxation period about fifteen minutes before the start. To become hyperactive or to manipulate yourself deliberately into an aggressive mood is mistakenly thought by many athletes to be a necessity. In reality, it only lowers their level of concentration. The decision to be aggressive on the course can be made calmly and shouldn't show in your behavior before starting. But to stand around quietly and freeze isn't advisable either. Get away from the hectic start atmosphere, exercise loosely, keep warm, breathe slowly and deeply, and clearly recall the few points you want especially to concentrate on. Now you are ready to go to the start to perform well and ski the best you can.

Tactics and Intuition

Every sport has its own tactics, but what is basically meant by "tactics"? One could say that it is a scheme that contains a competitor's well-calculated plans, but that is still flexible, liable to variation and, most of all, to intuition.

Phil Mahre

If you take part in a race you naturally hope for the best result possible. But on the day of the race you should never think about your hoped-for result. You're there to ski as well as you possibly can. At the start your mind and your full concentration must be on the course, the snow, the speed, your tactics, the intimate pleasure you feel when competing, and on your skiing.

When studying the course and the terrain you must work out a kind of battle plan. Setting up such a plan requires creative power, experience, and routine. You should imagine certain situations and how you will most probably behave in them. This will enable you to decide what kind of technical approach you will use.

It is very important to study and to recognize the character of a course. Is it fast or slow? Where are the rhythm changes? In slalom as in giant slalom you will never find a course that is exactly set in a regular rhythm. It is essential to realize this fact in order to adapt mentally to the rhythm changes when you ski a course. For this reason I consider a conditioning program with music, where your motions are bound to a beat, not necessarily good for a ski racer. It's not necessary to learn every single combination by heart in a slalom or giant slalom. Doing so could lead to tenseness and great limitation of your intuition. Also figuring out exactly where you will ski in a gate has only limited value. Most likely you won't be there anyway, if you really ski full-out, taking the necessary risks really to ski your best. But memorize and prepare for the few special situations you have noted while studying the course. An older and very experienced athlete will usually benefit more from studying a course a long time. Karl Schranz spent three hours inspecting the GS course when he became world champion at Val Gardena, Italy, in 1970.

At the same world championships, another racer won a gold medal, partially because of creative observation leading to good tactics. It was the twenty-year-old Swiss racer Bernhard Russi. He had number 15 and it had snowed a couple of inches overnight. Hundreds of people prepared the DH again before the start, so it had a beautiful smooth surface. In training the racers had faced a sheet of ice the whole week. Shortly before the start, Russi decided to ski a more direct line in the turns than he had in training. The course was a lot slower, and there was no need for being as high as when it had been icy and much faster. It was to an extent this smart tactical plan that brought Bernhard Russi this great victory.

In downhill you must make up your mind long before the race starts where your line is, where to start your turns, and where you will stay in your tuck. Otherwise, uncertainty will haunt you and even prevent you from sleeping the night before the race. Doubt and uncertainty about the trail easily meld with fear, and have ruined the sleep of many a racer. Downhills have to be inspected very carefully and over and over again. Like Russi, you must be able to adapt your plans to any changes in the course or conditions. In bad visibility you will be particularly grateful for the time you took really to study the terrain and the bumps in a course. This is all true for slalom, giant slalom, and downhill.

To recognize a course that is especially appealing and suited to you because of successful memories can be very beneficial. Gustavo Thoeni, the ultimate calculator, is, more than any other racer, able to make the right decision at the right time. In the 1974–1975 season he practically didn't train any DH at all. Still, he raced in some of them in order to gather the World Cup points the combined results of the top races offered. Even so he ended up as the only real challenger to Franz Klammer, who won eight out of nine downhills (once he fell). The scene was Kitzbühel, where 40,000 Austrians came to see Franz Klammer win. He had number 1 and risked everything, as usual, setting a new course record, although only a miracle saved him from a disastrous fall after a grave mistake near the finish line. No one in the first group beat him, and horrible falls were the terrible spectacle of the 40,000 live spectators and the estimated 20 million television viewers.

But at the start there was still a man for whom the race wasn't over: Gustavo Thoeni! He had already jokingly reminded Klammer and the other downhill specialists to wait until he was down. He had number 17, which is a good draw in the second group. Shortly before he left the starting gate he said to his coach, "Today it's worthwhile; it's difficult and fast. I'm going for it!" That was his reaction to Klammer's new record. With complete confidence in his technique, Thoeni had a perfect run and was beaten by Franz Klammer by only 3/1000 of a second. He had judged the situation right; it was his kind of conditions and course. Had it been slow and soft, he would have had a difficult time placing in the top ten among the world's best downhill specialists, who usually do well in slow conditions, since they have trained on soft snow for weeks. But every winter offers one or more fast icy downhills, where a superb technical skier like Gustavo can win.

Intuition plays a big role with the winning racer. Despite all your plans, you must feel your skis and let them run. Being too much on your edges can be a tactical or technical mistake. Intuition and natural feeling for the snow and the skis will help you correct bad tactics after a few gates. You must be able to feel whether the line you have chosen is fast, and if it is not, you must change it as soon as you can. My friend the late Spider Sabich, twice professional world champion, told me once with amazing frankness over a dinner table: "Sometimes it almost blows my mind when I see what some of those younger guys on the circuit are doing on skis. But I can still beat them, because I carry speed well. I like going fast and this is more a mental game than a matter of plain technique and physical condition." His words highlighted his competitive spirit and intuition rather than tactics, plans, and techniques.

On the day of competition, to avoid unnecessary stress situations, get up early, eat properly and sufficiently, and have enough time to study the course. Get accustomed to irregular mealtimes. If your start is at 12:30 P.M., don't go and swallow a cheeseburger and french fries at noon. A couple of chocolate bars at 11:30 will do, taking your hunger away and supplying you with some extra energy. Above all keep your hands away from drugs. Unless in your daily life you have been accustomed to them to a certain degree or are addicted in some form, their effect on your performance is rather negative. In case of a bad accident, certain drugs are even perilous if an immediate operation is urgently needed. Also, it is simply an unfair test if you try to use a drug to compete better, for one of the basic sports rules is to compete under the most equal conditions possible.

On the other hand, there are remedies that increase your fitness and help you to keep your regularity in your hectic life as a racer. A harmless soporific or pill against insomnia is better than a sleepless night. The change of food following races from country to country or state to state may cause irregularities in your digestion. Instead of feeling uneasy, why not get rid of this problem with the help of a weak laxative? Of course, this should not become a habit.

Courage and Fear

Courage and fear are connected; they stand opposite one another, but they can't stand alone. When you have experienced courage and fear, in downhill racing, you certainly know what I mean. There is no question that people show great individual differences in the way they handle their fears and in how they apply their courage. To an extent it's a question of your character. For a ski racer it is of utmost importance how he overcomes his fear with his courage. A racer must develop good judgment and good intuition in order to deal with courage and fear. It's common knowledge that fear and courage, poorly balanced, can bear tragic consequences for an athlete. Quite a few ski racers have had accidents because they couldn't admit their fear feelings. They tensed up in the starting gate and aimed hopelessly for a bad crash. Therefore, let's make an inventory of fear-related feelings and factors that are typical for ski racers.

1. Bad physical condition and the resulting symptoms of fatigue and exhaustion commonly cause fear. This is usually connected with a bad conscience because of lack of physical training. These are a couple of the main reasons for fear in all sports.
2. Insufficient technique to meet the difficulties in the course can easily create fear. Very often, and particularly in downhill, this may be the result of the limited possibilities for DH training in

A young racer builds up his courage at the International Training Camp in Alagna, Italy

the busy ski areas of today, with their tricky moguls made by the short-ski fan.

3. You can get psyched out by your fellow competitors racing down in your face in a breathtaking way at 60 miles an hour. Sometimes older and experienced racers delight in teasing and provoking their younger rivals in this way.

4. Lack of detailed knowledge of the course, particularly in bad visibility, leads to uncertainty and fear. Keep away from taking chances before you know the course really well in downhill.

5. The surprise at higher speeds on race day because of better course preparation, weather conditions, better wax, etcetera, can be unsettling.

6. A small fear can grow into a big fear. Tense muscles are the immediate result of cramped breathing. Tight muscles limit your feeling for balance. For instance, a tightrope walker would immediately fall off the rope if he became tense. Again, only conscious relaxation can solve this problem.

7. Fear of the slalom poles is more common than most people know.

8. Fear of failure, uncertainty, lack of self-confidence, and low self-esteem are often connected with the examples above, but not always.

9. In some cases an athlete may fear the responsibility of winning. This kind of fear is mainly mental and is very hard to overcome.

Let's think over some of these problems and try to find the proper answers. To begin with, I'm sure there is nothing more important than being absolutely fit. Fitness backs up the self-esteem and confidence you need for downhill racing as well as for managing extremely difficult and fast sections in a GS or slalom.

You can have confidence in your technique only when you have slowly built it up with many hours of practice. I have already described how to train specifically for downhill in the section "Downhill" on page 61.

It's not good for a racer to hang around on a DH course too long. Take one really good look, maybe watch the best racers once. That's enough! Now it's your turn! Onlookers usually get too impressed by the speed and flights of their competitors and consequently damage their self-confidence.

Always try to learn a downhill course as well as possible. If you know a downhill well you can ski full-out even in relatively bad light. Remember that many downhill races are held with poor visibility. If the weather is really bad, don't worry; they will postpone or cancel the training or race. If for some reason you do not know the course well, just ski it easily in a relaxed upright position even if the light is good. After one or two runs, you will know it well enough to start really going fast.

Unexpected extra speed on race day is fairly normal. You must accept and welcome these higher speeds. Above all, don't assume a higher position or break out of your tuck more than you did in training, even if you are afraid. After all, speed is the name of the game!

Pay great attention to the principle "tension needs relaxation." Whenever you find a short moment in a hairy DH to relax and breathe calmly a few times, do it. Not only will you tank up energy, but you will also find a better concentration level to face a tricky or even a dangerous situation. In very physically demanding sections, try to relax the muscles you aren't using. Doing so will help you balance well and let your skis run as fast as they can.

If a racer is afraid of slalom poles, he usually has plenty of reason. Most of the time he or she is a bad technician, and the well-justified fear of poles results from cutting too close with the ski tips, causing hooked tips, bad bruises all over, even a broken leg or sprained ankle. See page 55 in the technical part for a full description on how to solve this problem.

But fear of slalom poles can also be caused by training with poles that are too heavy and thick. For this very reason I tried training with extremely thin hazelnut poles in my camp at Alagna, Italy. They were about the diameter of a finger and brightly painted blue and red. At the end of the camp, with each racer training about 500 gates per day, we counted 200 broken poles, but we had no injuries despite the fact that the racers took a lot of chances during the whole camp. Even hooking the first gate in a flush didn't really hurt them beyond a hard landing. Not being afraid of the poles didn't encourage them to cut closer at all. It merely eliminated their fears, thereby helping them ski faster. After the first few misjudgments, each racer developed a better eye for how close he or she could cut a gate while still brushing it slightly with his or her inside arm.

Fear of failure haunts all racers, even the best. A high level of self-confidence helps you face this fear. Really training hard and intelligently so that you ski well, setting realistic goals for yourself, and a certain easy-goingness are the best ways to gain self-confidence. After doing this you can go to the starting gate and ski the best you can, despite your fear of failing.

There are some people who fear the responsibility of winning. They often take stupid risks with no chance of finishing, make "silly" mistakes on their second run of slalom, or just keep coming in second or third; even though everyone knows they could win. These racers must realize their fears and then logically defeat them. They must realize that they would not alienate their friends by winning. Indeed, they would only gain additional respect. You must be willing to face the depression of defeat after the euphoria of winning. Racing is full of ups and downs, but if you love your sport just for what it is, you will be able to face all the good and bad times philosophically. Unfortunately, the heavy pressure put on a winning racer by his parents, his friends, the press, and his coaches often makes athletes afraid to win. However, you just can't let onlookers spoil the fun of winning for you. With courage and confidence in yourself as a person, you can face the pressure and criticism when you lose. After all, it's only you who is racing. Someone has to win. Why shouldn't it be you?

You must clearly realize the source of your fear. Knowing is half the battle. Every racer has to overcome a certain amount of fear every so often. After admitting it you will find it much easier to solve your problems through courage, technical skills, and tactics. You absolutely should not ignore your fear feelings. As a natural protection, they are certainly necessary, preventing people from accidents and helping them realize their limits. Of course, some middle course has to be found. Don't be foolish and take crazy unnatural chances to prove your courage. Don't pay tribute to subconscious fear, particularly when it is not justified by the course. I know racers who were completely unaware of braking and standing up until they saw themselves on video. Subconscious fear is often the barrier a racer has to lift in order to become better. The only way to deal with it is to let it come out, admit it, and then defeat it. Together with your intuition and good judgment, you must mobilize your courage to overcome your fear.

What can we say about courage specifically? Do we have a chance to influence it? I strongly believe so. Courage is a kind of self-confirmation. Everyone knows how great you feel the moment after a true challenge of your courage. "I made it" is followed by relief, pleasure, and a certain pride. Each time your courage is successfully tested, it also gets strengthened. Let's say someone is truly afraid of jumping off a diving board, has never done it before, but is a fairly good swimmer. Some day he'll go onto the diving board and dive for the first time into the water. Following this, he gets out and dives over and over again. Later he will challenge himself to make his first somersault and so on. What suddenly happened? The dives are obviously connected to each other. By overcoming his fear of diving, the swimmer has increased his self-confidence and basically feels a lot more secure when diving. This gave him the new basis from which he could do new dives he never dreamed of before. A real achievement in courage may support you in facing even heavier dangers.

This opens the possibility of actually training your courage in some way. Read the section "Coordination, Courage, and Balance" to learn different ways to build up your courage. Use your imagination. Create all sorts of small tests for your courage. The characteristics of these tests has to be as follows. When you fail, it has to cause you some pain, like when falling on your stomach or back off the diving board. You must also be a little afraid, but carefully keep this within

Leith Lende

sensible limits and use your judgment. Never push so far that you really get injured in such tests.

Support each other when you are psyched out, with a good team spirit and mutual encouragement. Don't feel shy about bringing the subject up in the form of a discussion. It's advisable to do this in a group. This way, the individual athlete will be able to accept criticism without getting embarrassed and personally hurt in his pride. A coach should talk about his own experiences and frustrations with anxiety and courage, using both good and bad examples. This way, the athletes will be able to learn that they are not alone with their fears and anxieties; even their coach had them.

133

Learning and Correcting

You should set yourself a goal from time to time; this goal will differ from racer to racer. Then you have to put a lot of work, love, and willpower into your training to learn the new skills necessary to reach your goal. As I pointed out in the section "Why Racing? Impulses and Motives," in order to use your willpower in training and competition, you must first know exactly what you want to use it for. Only then can you apply your willpower properly.

During your apprenticeship to become a great ski racer, you'll have many moments of stagnation. Then you need creative imagination to see yourself skiing differently than you do. Sometimes it first takes an improvement in your physical condition to get yourself physically ready to ski differently. You have to learn how to improve your physical condition before you can get in better shape. Unfortunately, being told what you have to change is often not enough. Your coach may tell you as many times as he wants, "What you're doing is wrong, you should ski this way. . . ." without his criticisms having any effect. Sometimes it's just the end of the road unless a new concept comes into your view of ski racing. The absolutely best possible influence on your skiing is the live demonstration of a world class skier. This is the best teacher, and if you have time to see a top race, go and watch it. Study one detail at a time: for instance, the pole plant, then the early edge-set. It's incredible what a great impact watching the best can have on your own skiing. You may know how watching Jimmy Connors, Stan Smith, Arthur Ashe, or Billie Jean King play a match rubs off on your own tennis game with amazing results. **135**

Correction through anticipation
Steve and Phil Mahre not only look alike; they also ski alike. They ski similarly to the top Italians on the World Cup. This photo is of great technical value. It shows Phil in a tricky gate in the 1976 Senior Nationals at Copper Mountain, Colorado. He went full out and skied extremely fast into this off-set gate. Indeed his line was a little too direct, but he came out beautifully without losing any time. Let's look at what he did that saved him. First of all, he bent his body toward the fall line, putting tremendous pressure onto his lower ski. He simultaneously planted his pole well angulated. The pole is actually slightly bent. What more is there to say? Imagine what would have happened if he had bent forward at his waist, thereby putting pressure onto his ski tips instead of underneath his feet. Where would his tails have gone?

In the 1974-1975 season I closely watched how Greg Jones turned a nasty injury of his shoulder into a fascinating learning process and experience. He used his time watching his competitors race on the World Cup. He knew of his troubles with his pole plant. When Greg skied his first slalom after four frustrating weeks on the sidelines, he had a fine pole plant similar to that of the best Italians. Even the best make mistakes and have their specific weaknesses. Recognize your mistakes clearly in order to correct them successfully.

Here a good coach can be a great help. He must logically explain your mechanical or technical errors and faults in a plain straightforward way. A coach who does not explain and just keeps giving instructions is definitely on the wrong track because he only makes his athletes totally dependent on him. An athlete can be independent only if he becomes an expert at his sport. I believe that a strong streak of independence is one of the main characteristics the top ski racers have in common. It's both an unrewarding and bad approach for a ski coach to try to develop uniform ski racers. Individual advice concerning learning and correction is absolutely necessary. It's one of a coach's main occupations to criticize constructively a racer's training and races. This criticism has to come regularly and be reliable. A racer feels overlooked without response from his coach, particularly when he skis badly. He might even conclude that the coach has given him up. The right timing, a certain discretion, and the place where a coach makes his criticism are very important. Tact and intuition are what a coach needs here. Following is some advice to coaches on how to criticize their racers.

1. In most cases you should use a positive form of criticism.
2. When a coach criticizes, he must not exaggerate and embarrass the racer.
3. A good coach can picture himself making the same mistake. He must wonder how he can make the racer become conscious of his mistake.
4. A good coach should not get down on the racer personally. It's only the racer's outside form, his physical motions, or the

summary of the facts that led to his bad result that you criticize.

5.   Sometimes a racer needs a hard word. Maybe he was lazy or careless, or did a bad job preparing his skis, or maybe he took a foolish risk without a chance of succeeding. These flaws need firm criticism.

6.   A coach must become aware of the reasons or motives for his athlete's failures. Often you find that personal sorrows, lack of confidence, or the wrong goals are mental barriers for athletes. Here it takes personal care and sympathy for each athlete if a coach really wants to help successfully.

In some senses the human brain can be compared to a computer, which, fed with the wrong information, delivers the wrong answers. Only corrections planned to the last detail and proper instructions will lead to reliable results. The same is true for your brain. The brain notes little difference between thought-out motion and physically experienced motion. It just registers the message as one experience. It certainly helps a racer to correct a mistake successfully when on his way up the ski lift, while eating breakfast, or when warming up in the morning, he keeps thinking over and over again how to really ski well. But don't forget to give your mind a rest every once in a while. A rested mind is much more receptive and capable of finding a creative approach to correcting your mistakes.

Coaches, Racers, Relationships

Great champions, such as Thoeni, Killy, and Annemarie Moser-Proell, showed an unusual capacity for standing alone. They kept on winning despite the enormous stress that went with being a champion. A good coach must carefully prepare his top athletes to be able to take success with all its side effects. There are many examples of athletes who have won one big race, to their own surprise, and then couldn't take the pressure and responsibility this victory brought them. They simply weren't prepared for it. To build up confidence on a realistic basis is an important occupation, and probably one of the most difficult ones a coach has. He has to spot when an athlete is ready to win and then tell the athlete that.

Since there is a long climb to the top for any ski racer, you have to prepare him for that, too. When he really likes skiing, you can tell him that it will take about five to six years to become really good, and that he should build his educational plans solidly into his plans to become a top racer.

One of the most beautiful sides of coaching certainly is your communication with the athlete as a human being. This includes the coach's role in teaching the athlete other valuable things for his life besides purely ski racing facts. Sometimes this is a major occupation for a coach. Too often an athlete is confronted with parents who are overambitious and pushy, and who see their kids as future Olympic champions. As a coach you are confronted with such parents, whether you like it or not. I personally recommend that a coach ride the chairlift more often with kids suffering from this difficult type of parents. Naturally and in an easygoing manner you should talk and chat about the real values of sports. In a way, you substitute for the kind of father or mother that kid has always desired but has never had.

When I talk about the coach, I mean mainly the person who has the closest contact with the athlete. This may sometimes be the director of a program. The following pages describe good characteristics and even necessities for a good coach-athlete relationship.

A coach must try hard to be as impartial and unprejudiced as possible. Too often coaches develop and show their preferences for certain types of individuals, based upon personal attitudes and feelings. Regardless of your natural personal feelings, you should treat all your athletes equally and fairly.

A coach should provide a good image for his pupils of living style. He must be able to identify with the athletes and should not take advantage of his privileges in lodging, food, or travel. To a great extent, he must be willing to join the athletes in a clean, disciplined way of living.

A coach must help the individual athlete set his goals correctly. He has to advise each athlete to set his goal so that it is reachable with good effort.

Authority should not be forced upon the athlete. Discipline has to come out of confident leadership. Mutual trust and confidence between the coach and his athletes are essential. Yet he has to feel when hardness and severity are necessary and when tolerance is the right way to handle a problem. A coach must realize that a good ski racer is entitled to a certain freedom. Therefore, don't make narrow-minded rules. Your good image and your teaching should take care of any disciplinary problems.

Sometimes an athlete needs the complete discretion of a coach in a difficult personal matter. As a coach, you must listen to proposals from your athletes. Maybe they are good. Sometimes you might even have to correct your own ideas about a subject.

It is important that a coach be neutral and give each athlete hints on how he can contribute to his own program. Last but not least, a coach should try to form a strong team and to create an atmosphere conducive to a good team spirit. He must be the mediator between individuals. If necessary, he must end conflicts among teammates with certainty.

A coach must be frank and straightforward. He must admit the mistakes that he makes, such as slow wax, or bad tactical advice, so that the athlete doesn't incorrectly identify himself with a bad result. You will be surprised how you will gain the athlete's respect by admitting your mistakes. On the other hand, a coach has to make his comments and criticisms after each training and race to everyone. Sometimes this takes a lot of time, but it is absolutely necessary. The athlete expects the coach's comment whether it's positive or negative. Therefore, do it with the necessary tact and at the right moment.

A good coach never gets carried away into taking the credit for the good performances of his athletes. He may show his pleasure **139** about the good results of his athletes, but he must always give the individual the credit for his achievements. Otherwise, an athlete could rightfully feel cheated about his good performance. Naturally he enjoys being responsible for his victory.

Perhaps the most important point of all is that the coach must give his athletes correct advice and clear explanations of their mistakes. He must also inspire his athletes to train hard and to improve constantly. In the end this is what makes a successful team. A coach should always try to keep up with the latest technical and physical conditioning trends. However, he must be careful to separate the wheat from the chaff.

These are just a few points on the long list of talents a good coach must have. To find a man with the qualities described is not easy. Most of the men who could fill such demanding positions go into other professional fields simply because being a ski coach doesn't pay well enough. Even on the top level, associations have difficulties in finding the right men. A top Swiss expert once made a peculiar remark when he was asked to become head Swiss coach. He said, "I don't want to be the most poorly paid man on the entire team." In the meantime the situation may have changed slightly, but the salaries are still low, and it's hard to find properly educated and experienced coaches. The transition from racing to coaching has been made by quite a few former aces. But in most cases coaching is not their main occupation, because they have to feed a family. Again, this is a warning for racers who mistake ski racing for a long-term career. In most cases it isn't.

It's not just the coach who has to be alert and sensitive to mold a good team. Indeed, to a great extent it's you, the athlete! Here I want to give you some hints on how to establish a good understanding with your coach and how to become an asset to your team. These efforts can only be to your advantage in becoming a good racer.

Treat your coach with respect, and be tolerant. He may not be the perfect ski racer any longer, yet he may still be competent and able to teach and demonstrate to you "how to turn them." Every coach has his strong and weak points, but everyone can give you something, if you're able to catch it. I think it's a good thing to get to know different coaches and different methods of teaching. One coach can't possibly know everything. All champions in ski racing trained with more than one coach before they reached the top. There is nothing worse than excessively dogmatic coaching. You must not get attached to one opinion only. Constantly develop your own knowledge of ski racing and communicate with your coach about your searches and the ideas you have found.

A good team spirit is a wonderful thing to experience and be a part of. But it takes help from all the individuals involved. If you want to support a good friendly atmosphere, you must be tolerant and overlook certain differences in your teammates' outlooks and attitudes. They might not agree with you, either, on some subjects. Why argue and cause bad feelings when it's not necessary? On the other hand, it's great if you can establish communication with your teammates based on common interests. Sometimes you may even be the inspiration for a new recreational activity. If you have a good idea for the team, carry it out.

To be an egotist is definitely to your disadvantage. Egotism is a state of mind in which you mainly think about yourself. Dr. Otto Neumann writes in his book *Sports and Personality,* "Egotism originates in the desire of the individual to feel set off . . . or in other words to feel better." Many young successful athletes slide into this dangerous attitude because of inappropriate glorification of their early results. To an extent, this can again be the bad influence of pushy parents or even bad coaches. It's important for you to know that an egotist tends to refuse even constructive criticism. Without creatively responding to the corrections of your coach, you can't make it to the top. Humility is an important quality in a racer's character to make him able to receive new ideas and to improve his skiing. As a lone wolf on a disorganized team, you can hardly develop your skills. You lack enthusiasm, and above all, sound competition. That a good team spirit enhances the performance of the individual is well demonstrated by the best teams on the World Cup circuit.

Help your coach carry out his timetable and never be late.

Despite the friendship there may be between a coach and his **141** athletes, the coach must keep a certain distance from his team. The athletes must feel the sincere sympathy of their coach, but this certain distance from the team is one of the main necessities for good coaching.

When you feel uneasy and uncomfortable with some of your teammates, coaches, or other associates, think of what Edward Kennedy once said: "It takes two to have a lasting peace, but only one to take the first step."

Injury-Prone Ski Racers

It would be foolish to see a psychological reason behind all injuries, but, on the other hand, the average person usually sees injuries as accidents or bad luck. This may also be true. When a racer has injured himself a few times in a row people say, "He is caught in a chain of bad luck." Someone else may remark, "Oh well, he is

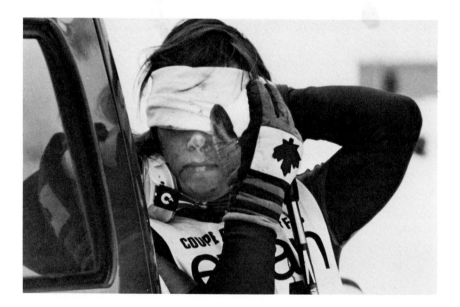

accident-prone!'' I've never heard anyone give any further explanation of what is ''accident-prone,'' but the term is right. There are
indeed injury-prone ski racers. To an extent, I may have been one
myself. During my years of racing and coaching, and after analyzing
my own experiences, I became aware of a few typical tendencies
among the ski racers who get injured. The reason for this section is to
draw the attention directly of those individuals who may have such
problems.

I will list below some of the characteristics and reasons for athletes
to be injury-prone. If you recognize yourself in one or more examples,
then it's necessary for you to be careful and to work out your problems
somehow before you get hurt. There is no doubt in my mind that if
you can identify with some of the following points that you are in
danger of getting hurt.

1. Some racers literally want to be injured. It's their easy way
   out. ''He needed a crutch'' is a popular saying and indirectly
   related to such athletes.
2. Escaping into an injury because an athlete feels pressured is
   more common than many people believe. After all, who
   doesn't remember getting sick shortly before a tough test in
   school? In ski racing, the consequences of such an attitude
   may have disastrous physical results.
3. ''You are a fearless tiger'' may be the comment that leads
   you into taking foolish risks while trying to live up to your
   reputation. No longer do you use your healthy instinctive
   judgment. You are a daredevil and are expected to take the
   craziest lines, which are not necessarily the fastest.
4. You are afraid of competition. Maybe you think you will be
   beaten. You don't really trust your skiing abilities and feel
   inferior to other competitors. A slight injury at the right moment prevents you from competing and looking bad.
5. Ski racers who tend to work on their strengths instead of their
   weaknesses, for instance on their DH position instead of on
   their high-speed curves, are usually injury-prone. In reality,

143

they know about their problems, but their false pride doesn't allow them to work on their weaknesses and makes them ski beyond their limits.

6. Some racers wear big bandages or braces, sometimes maybe a little too big, which are obviously good to catch the eye of the coach or of other people the athlete is associated with. The athlete feels that he may be admired for his guts to continue racing despite pain and injury. But such small crutches easily develop into big ones. Suddenly athletes may fake a bigger injury. Their grimaces have no relationship to their actual pain. They are obviously seeking attention. Such behavior can easily set the stage for a really nasty accident where you truly get attention afterward. But is it worthwhile?

7. Pressure from parents has manipulated many a young racer into an accident. A father who sets goals that are far beyond the reach of his child, and enthusiastically tries to have his son accept them, truly does him a bad service. The young racer who believes that his father's love for him will be fulfilled only by future top results is easily tempted to get injured. In this way, the child will never have to come to the actual test, and the young racer will never be confronted with his limits, which may fall below his father's goals for him. The pressure is off. The father suddenly shows concern and gives his injured kid a lot of loving attention. That's usually what the kid was looking for in the first place. Parents who want their kids to make it on their terms shouldn't be surprised to find their youngsters in the hospital someday. It is often the kids' way of saying that they can't take the unrealistic pressure put on them by their parents.

A serious injury usually has a negative influence on your psychological inner self, and sometimes it takes a long time to over-come your fears in order to ski as well as you did before the accident. It's beyond my capabilities to offer you much specific advice on how to deal with injury-causing tendencies. Indeed, this in an extremely individual, difficult, complex, and sometimes painful procedure. In some cases the best advice may be to quit ski racing rather than to be injured over and over again. To change to a less dangerous field of sports might not be a bad idea for some athletes. On the other hand, I hope that the examples I have mentioned will give an injury-prone athlete some understanding and insight into his problem.

Many great ski racers, even world champions and Olympic medal winners, have had serious injuries. However, to my knowledge neither Toni Sailer, Jean-Claude Killy, Gustavo Thoeni, nor Annemarie Moser-Proell has ever faced a really serious accident. Along with luck, they obviously must have excellent judgment, which, along with being in top physical shape, is the best protection against injuries. It was not purely accidental that they never were seriously hurt.

Racing and Education

Since ski racing is a sport that is connected with continual traveling, often over long distances, one can immediately forecast a collision with the normal school system. In some alpine countries, strong efforts have been made to provide education for racers with growing talents. But the subjects taught by these experimental schools are mostly directed toward a physical education major. Why should a great skier necessarily become a physical educator? Where does the young talented racer go who is good in languages or math, or who wants to become a doctor or engineer yet would still love to race full-out for a while? These are difficult questions, and appropriate future solutions would require a great amount of money. Following are a couple of examples of world class racers who are or recently were on the World Cup circuit.

A top German competitor who was winning World Cup races was kicked out of medical school. He wasn't a bad student, but he was not a brilliant one, either. The professors had no understanding for what he was up to: trying to be a top ski racer and becoming a doctor at the same time. He chose to continue racing. But will there be an opening again in medical school after his ski career has ended?

Another world class racer said to me, "I think that today's racer unfortunately lives totally for his sport. It's his obsession, and he has no time for other things. This is no good for your soul, your spirit, or for life in general. Personally I often take walks in the forest, and my main occupation is the beautiful profession of a wood-carver and sculptor. I'm fortunate, but I know some that weren't. I think it's important that every young racer sees that it will be all over one day. This would help him ski in a more easygoing way and enjoy the competition for what it is. I'm a little down on coaches in general. They have the opportunity to point out the real values of the sport; instead they simply glorify points and results. Often they even judge individuals because of a tenth of a second. That's when it really gets bad. . . . As the situation stands, it is totalitarian program directors who are the preferred ones and who usually produce successful teams. To leave space for individual desires, to allow slower development for educational or special reasons, and to pay attention to a difficult character often don't fit into their concepts. Many racers with real potential struggle to a stop right here."

Despite a lot of people who believe differently, I am convinced that if someone has a strong desire to ski race and truly loves it, he can complete a good education and perfect his skiing at the same time. Others may stop school and just race after high school for a year or two in order to "give it a full try." This may not be so bad if the particular racer has an imaginative nature and takes out enough time for his education and other activities. Otherwise he may easily get bored and could become stale. After a year he may give up, frustrated by his lack of success "with so much training." No matter how many hours a day you spend training, it's still the years of regularity in conditioning and skiing, paired with an alert conception while training, that enables you to become a top athlete.

Skiing in itself on a top level can be a great education. At least, it was for me. It can teach you lots of things that are really worthwhile knowing. Your travels and friendships with people from other parts of the world can teach you about other cultures: their food, entertainment, customs, attitudes, money, and methods of doing things. With a little effort, you can even learn other languages. You can learn a lot about yourself and how you react in stressful situations. You can develop yourself and strengthen your character. You can have a hell of a time. Keep your eyes open and an open mind, and you'll find ski racing is a great addition to your education.

Above all I would like to say: Don't neglect your formal education, no matter how strong the call to race may be for you. Maybe you will take a break of a year or two from school. But never forget that ski racing is not a career, even when the top pros and best amateurs make quite a bit of money from racing.

Unknown racer at the World Championships at St. Moritz, 1974

A Few Hints
on Equipment

Equipment Purchase

Let me give you some advice on buying your equipment. As the son of a big ski retailer in Zurich, Switzerland, I have been around sports equipment all my life. I used to go to the big ski factories with my father to choose the expensive skis for our shop. We used to practice our own quality control at the highest level. "That ski has a bridge; it won't be fast" were words I became aware of at a very young age. Consequently, I never purchased a slow pair of skis for myself.

I also remember well how impressed I was watching my father testing those skis. He took a pair in his hands and flexed them, then he pressed them together in the middle to check that they closed and met nicely everywhere. Then he lifted one leg off the ground and set his foot onto the middle of the ski, applying some pressure to the ski, and looked from the tip to the tail. This is a simple but very effective method to discover whether a ski forms a perfectly straight and smooth line or if it has a "bridge." A bridge is a flat spot in the middle of the ski, interrupting the smooth line a ski should have from tip to tail. If a ski has a bridge, it will be slow and certainly won't hold on ice, even when it's well prepared. Another way to tell if a ski has a bridge is by flexing it. If the ski has a soft tip, a stiff center, and a soft tail, it has a bridge. Toward the tip your ski may bend a little, particularly a GS ski. Do these simple tests when choosing your skis. Just check them yourself right in the shop. You may know more about skis than the salesman, who might not even ski. Never buy too stiff a ski. A relatively flexible ski holds even on ice better than a stiff ski. In soft snow, in ruts, or in moguls, you are much better off with a relatively soft ski.

The present world class men use 203 cm. to 207 cm. slalom skis (actual length 200 cm. to 205 cm. respectively) and 207 cm. to 212 cm. giant slalom skis (actual length 205 cm. to 210 cm.). The exception is Ingemar Stenmark, who uses 203 cm. skis for both events, although his have different cuts and flexes according to the event and snow conditions. The world class women use 190 cm. to 195 cm. slalom skis and 195 cm., 200 cm., or 203 cm. giant slalom skis. Like the men's skis, their skis are actually 2 cms. to 3 cms. shorter than marked. In downhill, the research departments of the leading brands have developed skis for different snow conditions and pistes. The top male downhillers are using 220 cm. to 223 cm. skis (actual length 118 cm. to 221 cm.). The best women use 210 cm., 212 cm., or 215 cm. (actual length 208, 210, and 213 cm.) downhill skis. The ski length you use is a question of how big you are, how strong you are, and what you like. You can't avoid paying quite a bit for a good pair of skis. Each brand has its top models, and they are made a little more carefully than their less expensive lines. But you don't have to buy the most expensive skis. It's much more important that you buy a good pair that is well made with a good flex, according to your weight and the right length. Make the bridge test.

Make sure you buy a reputable pair of bindings. The most important thing about your bindings is to have them set properly. Ask your coach's advice on this point. When you mount your bindings, you should pay careful attention to where you put the toe piece. First you measure the cord length of your skis. The cord length is the direct line between the tip and the tail. Then you divide the cord length in half, and that measurement is the center of the ski.

The following advice refers to the place where the toe of your boot should be. Men and women with up to a size 9 boot should mount their slalom skis 1 cm. ahead of center, their giant slalom skis in the center, and their downhill skis 1 to 2 cm. back of center. When your boot is longer than 32 cm., measure the distance between 32 cm. and the actual boot length. Then you divide this distance in half and move your toe piece forward that amount. For example, a size 12 should be about 1 to 2 cm. ahead of normal. Now your ski is in balance again. With an extremely small foot (size 3 or 4), the only change you make is to mount your slalom skis only 0.5 cm. ahead.

A pair of good boots is almost of equal importance to your skiing as your skis. Only a high-quality product will do for a good skier. If you buy a relatively cheap boot, it will go to pieces in a short while. Take a look at the boots the best racers are using and buy something similar. It's not easy to advise you on the amount of forward lean you should use. Even the present world class racers are divided in their approach. Thoeni and Gros use very little forward lean in their boots, while Stenmark uses a fairly extreme forward lean. For a young racer I would rather recommend using neither extreme. You have to be in very good shape to use an extreme boot one way or the other.

In recent years many sports shops have started to offer their customers canting tests. Knowing that over 95 percent of all world class racers don't use cants, I can't hesitate in thinking that to a great extent it must be a purely business-oriented development in the ski industry rather than an actual help for the regular skier. Don't get me wrong. I saw racers cant their boots fifteen years ago. Former world champion Luggi Leitner from Germany canted his boots, but his bowed legs were similar to those of a professional cowboy! However, I sincerely doubt that many skiers need cants, and there are many skiers who would be better off not using any cants. But if you decide to cant your boots, do it only after careful observation and with an obvious reason. You must adapt the width of your stance constantly in order to ski on a flat ski. After all, you are already accustomed to using your legs the way they are naturally built. This constant natural adaptation to the right width in your stance is much more reliable than the computerized "miracle" cure of a cant machine.

When you buy a pair of ski poles make sure that your elbow forms an approximate right angle when you are standing erect in your ski boots.

Regarding clothing, I have little to say. Make sure you are warm and comfortable. In fast giant slaloms you should wear relatively aerodynamic ski wear. For downhill you definitely need a suit.

Ski Preparation

When you own a good pair of skis you must take care of them carefully. Only in this way will you get to know them really well, and they will repay you by performing beautifully. If you were to let two weeks pass without sharpening your edges, your skis would go from good to mediocre to bad, particularly when it is icy. This would also have a direct effect on your technique. You would adjust your technique to the poor shape your skis are in. Every top racer has a feeling for how his skis must be prepared. He knows how sharp an edge must be so that it holds well. The sharpness of your edges must be adjusted to the snow conditions.

Ski preparation also involves tactics and your way of approaching a race. Do you plan to ski full-out, directly and aggressively, round and smoothly, or something in between? Is the snow icy, soft, hard-packed, or mushy? You must decide how sharp you will make your edges according to these facts. When you ski well with a certain edge in certain snow you should remember how your edge felt, so that you can recall it when you face the same conditions again. The present national teams all have service reps who are professionals and prepare the skis perfectly for each race. However, most national team members are able to prepare a hell of a ski for themselves if they have to.

Indeed, they did it for many years before they reached the top. Only many years of experience and willingness to learn all about ski preparation and waxing will make you an expert. Unless you make these efforts, you may go into many a race with an unequal chance.

Many racers have stood in the starting gate with a two-second disadvantage solely because of how their skis were prepared. Below I list numerous points which you must pay attention to when preparing and waxing your skis.

1. First of all, watch an expert while he works on his skis. There is no better demonstration than seeing "live" how skis are prepared for an important international race.

2. If you work regularly on your skis, you will have to do only a little work each time. Five to ten minutes will usually suffice, and you will have a ski ready to race on or for a good training session.

3. When sharpening your edges, you must pay attention to the pointers I have already described. Furthermore, make sure you hold your file at a perfect right angle to the edge. There are several techniques used for filing edges. It is important that you work exactly and perfectly. You must get into it, and try to do a good job.

4. After filing your edges, you must smooth them and remove the burrs, as a final touch, with very fine emery paper or stone. Sometimes, particularly in soft snow, you don't want to have sharp tips, so you should dull the last foot of your tip more than the rest of the edge. You should carry emery paper with you when you ski so that you can dull your edges if the snow conditions are softer than you expected.

5. It is essential that you have smooth ski bottoms. Scratches and gouges must be fixed. There are many different ways of doing this. There is no excuse for not learning how to fix scratches so well that you can't tell where they were.

6. Before you apply any wax to your bottoms, all the old wax must be removed with wax remover manufactured by the wax companies. Only an absolutely clean bottom guarantees

that your wax will work properly. If you wax your skis often and never clean. your bottoms, the polyethylene base tends to suck up and retain wax. Consequently, the wax you apply for the race mixes with the undefined mixture on the bottom of your skis. There is no way you will be able to hit the right wax like this. Waxing on a completely clean bottom will give you a chance to develop a proper knowledge of fast wax mixtures. Before applying the wax onto the clean bases, it is advisable to roughen up the surface of your base with very fine emery paper, and then clean the base again.

7. There are several brands of wax. I use almost all of them. Some are better in new snow, others are better in old snow, and so on. Only a lot of practical experience can teach you what wax to use for different conditions.

8. First you have to heat up the proper wax combination in a pot and then apply it with a brush. If you aren't in a warm room it is sometimes necessary to iron the wax quickly after you have applied it with a brush. It's of utmost importance not to iron slowly, because you would only mix the proper wax combination with the impregnated wax you couldn't remove from your bottoms. Waxing has to be done quickly and with skill.

9. As you probably know, you get a really fast ski only when you leave just a thin film of wax on the bottoms of your skis by scraping the rest of the wax off with a well-prepared scraper. Prepare your tools well before you work on your skis. Every really good craftsman sharpens his tools before he goes to work. A poorly prepared scraper would leave nasty little lines in your bottoms when scraping the wax off.

10. Before you scrape, you must make sure that the wax has cooled off sufficiently. If you are sure what the weather is going to be like, you may put the wax on the night before the race and scrape in the morning.

11. In extremely soft and wet snow, you must get a lot of air under your skis. Besides using the right wax combination,

which you apply in the regular way, you should rub some plain dry yellow or other soft wax on top of the film of wax. This is very fast, when it's really wet, and you only need to ski in for 200 yards or less before the start.

12. In almost all snow conditions it is essential that you ski on your waxed skis before the start. How long you ski in depends on the snow conditions and temperatures as well as on the wax combination you applied. In cold weather and soft snow you may have to ski in for a couple hours to get your skis really fast. On ice you should only ski one half-run at the most, before the start.

A racer who always carefully prepares his skis will have a good chance to achieve consistent results. He knows his equipment, and he knows he can rely on his edges. He knows how his skis will react in the race. He doesn't have to be afraid of any particular ice plates, unlike someone who prepares his skis only for a race and never for training. Training on poorly prepared skis can harm your self-confidence. A few bad turns because of dull edges will automatically make you ski more cautiously, less aggressively, and therefore more slowly.

Final Word

Looking back at the contents of this book, I hope that you will gather a lot of good pointers and ideas from the many photos and also from my words. At the end I have to draw your attention to the continual development of ski racing. Keep your eyes open! I realize that we all have to search together for the answers of tomorrow, and not only in ski racing. We all know that. But for the time when we are doing it, ski racing is a great education, teaching us how to work extremely hard and to overcome many challenging situations. Before any of you becomes a top racer, he or she will have given a lot to the sport, with great idealism. This makes it worthwhile.

Finish!

Bibliography

Books:

Bear, Ruedi. *Technical Outlines for Ski Racing* (Wädenswil: Ruedi Bear Publication, 1974).

————. *Some Outlines and Advice for Young Racers* (Wädenswil: Ruedi Bear Publication, 1969).

————. *Psychologische Hintergrunde im Spitzensport* (Magglingen: Ruedi Bear Publication, ETS Magglingen, 1967).

Donath, Rolf, and Klaus-Peter Schüler. *Ernährung der Sportler* (Berlin: Sportverlag Berlin, 1972).

Editors of *Ski Racing. The Interview Book* (Denver: Paper House, Inc. 1974).

Gamma, Karl. *Ski Suisse* (Derendingen: Habegger Verlag).

Italian Ski Association. *Il Libro Dello Sci.*

Jäger, K., and G. Oelschlägel. *Kleine Trainingslehre* (Berlin: Sportverlag Berlin, 1974).

Joubert, Georges. *Teach Yourself to Ski* (Aspen: Aspen Ski Master, 1972).

Kaech, Arnold. *Magglinger Stundenbuch* (Bern: Paul Haupt Verlag, 1957).

Kemmler, Jürgen. *Perfektes Skitraining im Schnee + Zuhause* (Munich: BLV Verlagsgesellschaft, 1974).

Kemmler, Reiner. *Psychologisches Wettkampftraining* (Munich: BLV Verlagsgesellschaft, 1973).

Lorenz, Konrad. *Vom Weltbild des Verhaltungsforschers* (Munich: Deutscher Taschenbuch Verlag, 1968).

Martin, Paul. *Im Banne des Sport* (Zurich: Büchergilde Gutenberg, 1957).

Neumann, Otto. *Sport und Persönlichkeit* (Munich: Johann Ambrosius Barth, 1957).

Ogilvie, Bruce, and Thomas Tutko. *Problem Athletes and How to Handle Them* (London: Tafnews, 1966).

Pedersen, Tage. *Getting in Shape to Ski* (New York: Association Press, 1970).

Piderman, Guido. *Sportverletzungen und Schäden des Bewegungsapparates* (Bern: Sportmedizinische Schriftenreihe Wander, 1958).

Puni, A. Z. *Abriss der Sportpsychologie* (Berlin: Sportverlag Berlin, 1961).

Research and Teaching Papers of ETS Magglingen (Magglingen: Federal School for Physical Education, 1965–1967).

Schönholzer, G. *Probleme des Spezifischen Muskel Trainings* (Geneva: Editions Médecine et Hygiène, 1963).

Schultz, J. H. *Das Autogene Training* (Stuttgart: Grune, 1932).

Stockfelt, Torbjörn. *Leistungssteigerung im Sport* (Rüschlikon, Zurich: Albert Müller Verlag, 1972).

Thomas, Sim, Peter Looram, and Bill Harriman. *Aspen Coaches Report on Technical Outlines for Ski Racing* (Aspen: January 1975).

Yesudian, Selvarajan, and Elisabeth Haich. *Sport + Yoga* (Munich, Engelberg: Drei-Eichen-Verlag AG, 1972).

Magazines:

Jugend & Sport,
    Magglingen
Sci, Neve Sport, Milan
Ski, France
Ski Racing
Ski, Switzerland
Ski, USA
Skiing, USA
Sport, Zurich

Photograph Credits